"Meredith Gould has provided an excellent resource to those who believe that the future of mission lies in a world where networked lives and amplified humans await the proclamation of the Gospel. *The Social Media Gospel* offers a road map for those leaving the Church of the modern era behind for the adventurous missionary landscape of a social-structured world."

—The Rt. Rev. C. Andrew Doyle,
IX Bishop, Episcopal Diocese of Texas

"For those beginning to explore new technologies, those regularly engaging with social media, or for *anyone* who wants to communicate the good news to a new generation—*The Social Media Gospel* is crucial."

—Carol Howard Merritt,
author of *Tribal Church* and *Reframing Hope*

"Meredith Gould has poured her training as a sociologist, experience as a magazine writer, omnivorous appetite for social media, and passion for the Gospel into a book that should appeal to just about anyone who thinks about digital ministry. *The Social Media Gospel* is a valuable contribution from one of the best known thinkers in the field."

—Jim Naughton, editor of Episcopal Cafe
and co-author of *Speaking Faithfully:
Communications as Evangelism in a Noisy World*

"For those interested in mission and ministry in the newly-discovered, heavily-peopled, land of the internet, Meredith Gould's book on *The Social Media Gospel* is a must read. For those of us already active there, Meredith brings an invitation to reflect on what we are doing and ways to improve. For those new and uncertain—here is step-by-step advice from a skilled practitioner."

—Rev. Bosco Peters, www.liturgy.co.nz, @liturgy

"In the world of social media where so many proclaim themselves as 'how to' gurus, Meredith Gould breaks through the clutter and jargon. She uses simple language to help churches and pastors understand *why* social media is important and how to effectively use it as a tool for ministry. This book is for the beginner or those looking to go further with social media."

—Rev. Alan Rudnick, pastor, author, blogger,
and social media practitioner

"If your church is using social media or considering it, you need to read *The Social Media Gospel*. As a veteran sociologist, author, Twitter chat host, and lover of Christ and his church, there's no one better qualified to serve as your guide to church social media than Meredith Gould."

—Paul Steinbrueck, co-founder & CEO
of OurChurch.Com

"The Word is active and alive via social media, connecting minds and hearts through shared faith. While some church leaders fear exploring the digital mission field, people like Meredith Gould write groundbreaking books like this one, fearlessly and wisely leading the way to a truly new evangelization."

—Fran Rossi Szpylczyn, Catholic writer
and lay minister blogging at *There Will Be Bread*

"Meredith Gould answers the questions many church leaders and ministers have about the use of social media for ministry in her new book, *The Social Media Gospel*. A ministry insider and experienced user of social media, Meredith overcomes objections and eases fears with knowledgeable insights, good humor, and excellent end-of chapter reflection questions. *The Social Media Gospel* is a delightfully warm and welcoming invitation to share the Good News in new ways."

—Sister Susan Wolf, SND (@srsusan),
Founder and President of Catholic Web Solutions

The Social Media Gospel

Sharing the Good News
in New Ways

Meredith Gould

LITURGICAL PRESS
Collegeville, Minnesota

www.litpress.org

Cover design by Stefan Killen Design. Cover art © GL Stock Images and iStockphoto.

Scripture texts in this work are taken from the *New Revised Standard Version Bible* © 1989, Division of Christian Education of the National Council of the Churches of Christ in the United States of America. Used by permission. All rights reserved.

1   2   3   4   5   6   7   8   9

Library of Congress Cataloging-in-Publication Data

Gould, Meredith, 1951–
    The social media gospel : sharing the good news in new ways / Meredith Gould, PhD.
         pages   cm
    Includes bibliographical references and index.
    ISBN 978-0-8146-3558-2 (pbk. : alk. paper) —
ISBN 978-0-8146-3583-4 (e-book)
    1. Communication—Religious aspects—Christianity.   2. Social media.   I. Title.

BV4319.G67   2013
269'.2—dc23   2013010963

For all who boldly embrace new technologies
to build community and deepen faith.

Where two or three are gathered in my name,
I am there among them.

—Matthew 18:20

Contents

Foreword

Dear Pastor . . .

I probably know what you're thinking, sitting there with this book in your hands. Maybe someone on your leadership team recommended it to you; perhaps you got it for yourself to learn something new. However you started reading *The Social Media Gospel*, chances are your first thought was something along the lines of "I don't have time for this."

Home visits, hospital visits, sermon preparation, small groups, meetings, judicatory responsibilities—who has time for one more thing?! As a solo pastor of a midsize congregation, I understand. Time is both precious and at a premium.

However, you can't afford to continue to ignore social media. In one form or another, social media is here to stay. Social media is part of your congregants' lives, part of your community and neighborhood, and—whether you realize it yet or not—part of your ministry.

A few words as you begin this journey of learning about social media.

First, social media is not a replacement for face-to-face, in-the-flesh pastoral care. Social media can be an extension of a pastor's personal presence but will never entirely replace it. As you think about how social media can help your ministry, avoid either/or thinking. Instead of asking, "Should we do this online instead of how we currently do it?" ask, "How can online communications enhance the ways we're currently doing this ministry?"

Second, you don't have to be the expert for your congregation. I bet there are people in your congregation who know how to use social media. Enlist their help. Encourage them to use their gifts. Support them as they bring the church's presence onto social media. Be their cheerleader and advocate, and ask them how you can best contribute to the work.

Third, pastors who are online run into the same sort of boundary and confidentiality issues that pastors always run into. The rules of confidentiality that apply in the rest of your ministry also apply online. The ultimate privacy setting is not found in the user settings of Facebook or Twitter, but in your own heart. If you would not say it in public, don't put it online. Period.

Finally, be brave, be bold. In many ways, the church is blazing new paths with social media. Now is the time to do a new thing, to proclaim God's word in new and exciting ways. It is good to read about social media; it is good to think about how you're going to move forward. Sooner or later the time will come when you just have to take the plunge. *The Social Media Gospel* will help you!

Pastor, your job—whatever your denomination—is to proclaim the Gospel and to care for your flock. Social media is a set of tools that will *exponentially* increase your ability to do these key ministerial tasks. Social media is both a stethoscope, magnifying your ability to listen to your congregation and community, and a megaphone, magnifying your ability to proclaim God's word to your community.

I have been where you are—just beginning to learn about social media and think about how I could use these new tools to improve my ministry. I have helped others begin those same explorations. One of my first recommendations to church leaders is that they find someone to help guide them through these new technologies. You could not ask for a better guide than Meredith Gould.

In fact, Meredith was my own guide when I began exploring how to use social media for my ministry. Meredith is a communications professional and sociologist who understands how messages spread and how technologies work. But more importantly, she knows ministry. She works alongside many pastors and other professional church communicators. She understands the peculiarities of how we work and why we do this work. Like you, she is passionate about growing the kingdom and bringing the Gospel to the world.

You can easily find Meredith on social media platforms, talking about the Gospel and helping pastors and other leaders use social media effectively and well. She has earned a reputation as a go-to resource person for any of us who are trying to figure out why and how social media can help our ministries. She is also—as you will discover in these pages—a whole lot of fun.

God bless you, and your ministry, as you venture into the world of church social media!

> — Rev. David L. Hansen (@Rev_David)
> Pastor, St. John Lutheran Church of Prairie Hill
> Brenham, Texas

Preface

In my world of ministry, these two verses from Scripture are always bumping up against one another:

There is nothing new under the sun. (Eccl 1:9)

See, I am making all things new. (Rev 21:5)

Such is the practical reality of being called to the ministry of church communications in general and digital ministry in particular. As Christians, we are always called to share the Good News. Online technologies are simply the latest and greatest means available, delighting some and fraying the nerves of others. In this book I invite you to consider embracing social media to enhance your ministerial efforts as well as your own participation in the Body of Christ.

Most people use the term digital ministry to describe the growing use of online tools to share the Gospel and build church beyond the building. When I hear the term, I also think about ministering to those who reject digital technology because they think it's complicated, alienating, and otherwise antithetical to what it means to be and do church. *The Social Media Gospel: Sharing the Good News in New Ways* is my contribution to conversations that include but are not limited to addressing these questions:

- Why should ministers of the church, lay or ordained and regardless of ministerial call, bother with digital technology?

- If we believe God is everywhere and in all things, how can digital technology help us seek and find God?
- How can I persuade my sisters and brothers in Christ, especially those in positions of leadership, to use social media?

This is a book about why anyone in ministry ought to welcome digital tools to build community and deepen faith. It's absolutely *not* a guide to setting up social media accounts. You can easily find that information by searching Google or YouTube, if you prefer audio-visual tutorials. And I underscore the importance of going online to find current information because these platforms change constantly.

For example, in the month between turning in this book's manuscript and writing this preface, Facebook changed its timeline configuration at least three times and added structured status updates; Twitter rolled out Vine, a looping video application and sharing service; Pinterest added the option of opening business accounts, something that would work well for churches; and observers were finally getting around to writing screeds about Snapchat, a one-to-one sharing platform that transmits images that self-destruct after a user-determined time (up to ten seconds). By the time you read this book either in print or on an e-reader, new digital platforms will have emerged; familiar ones will have changed the way they look or how they work.

Ongoing, rapid change within digital platforms is, in part, what some church folk find so off-putting about social media. But while specific social media platforms change often and quickly, the basic principles guiding their usage are relatively durable. Here, in short stand-alone chapters I describe core principles for using social media strategically in the world of church:

Section I: Frameworks for Understanding offers ways to think more about social media within a variety of conceptual frameworks—theology, sociology, psychology, learning theory. The final chapter in this section expands my favorite meme, "virtual community is real community."

Section II: Choosing Social Media is where I explain the central importance of strategic planning and building community by generating participation; address concerns about abandoning print and bridging the digital divide; and then focus on major social media platforms in chapters descriptively titled "Why Choose. . . ."

Section III: Making Social Media Work includes chapters describing how to deal with what can but shouldn't get in the way of using social media wisely and well. In this section you'll find chapters about managing multiple platforms, online conflict, and burnout, as well as another favorite meme of mine, "church is not a building."

Each chapter includes questions for reflection to help you think through what works, what doesn't, and what could work better relative to using social media to build church and faith. I hope church leadership and groups—not just those involved with church communications—will use the "Thought Bytes" to grapple with whatever might be getting in the way of using these dynamic tools for twenty-first-century ministry. Those charged with strategic planning will find more specific, practical, and actionable suggestions in these appendixes: Strategic Choices; Yes, You Need a Social Media Policy; and The Communications Audit.

I'm also hoping you'll rejoice in the relative lack of footnotes. Although I have oodles of scholarly training, this is not an academic book. While clearly and inescapably informed by my training as a sociologist, everything I write about here is anchored in two major arenas of learning: (1) direct, in-the-trenches experience with every major social media platform and providing consulting services to local congregations as well as church judicatories across denominations; and (2) wisdom culled from interacting with participants in the weekly church social media

xvi   *The Social Media Gospel*

(#chsocm) chat on Twitter, an ecumenical chat I claim unholy bragging rights to having started in July 2011. Yea verily, social media has transformed my life and work.

After nearly six years of active, near-daily social media engagement in some form or another, I can honestly say that almost all of my closest friends, dearest colleagues, and most valued partners in ministry are in my life at this point thanks to digital technology. This is equally true in the secular world of healthcare communications, where my active digital involvement resulted in an invitation to serve on the External Advisory Board of Mayo Clinic's Center for Social Media (wonderful people of faith encountered there too!). Only a small percentage of these folks have I actually met face-to-face, but that hasn't prevented a shared sense of purpose from emerging and relationships from maturing. Come, Holy Spirit.

What you've probably already figured out and will discover in more detail is that I'm a passionate advocate for using social media tools for building community and deepening faith. Social media has made that possible for me. My prayerful hope is that social media becomes that for you and those you serve for the glory of God and Christ Jesus.

Shrove Tuesday, 2013

Acknowledgments

Digital technology has made it possible for me to receive almost daily counsel, encouragement, and inspiration from dozens, if not hundreds, of people, many of whom I may never meet in person. And so I happily broadcast global thanks to participants in these Twitter-based communities: church social media (#chsocm), chaplains on social media (#socmedchap), healthcare social media (#hcsm), and Mayo Clinic Center for Social Media (#mccsm).

For sanity-restoring laughter when ministry—digital and otherwise—gets frustrating, I've come to rely on @UnvirtuousAbbey and @JesusOfNaz316.

More specifically, I've been supported by a gaggle of guardian angels before, during, and after writing *The Social Media Gospel*. These dearly beloveds provided spiritual cheerleading as well as specific editorial input on early drafts: Rev. David Hansen (who also wrote the fine foreword), Ruth Harrigan (my steady Sherpa on three previous books), Brenda A. Keller (whose dark wit keeps me grounded), and the Rev. Joseph Smith (whose sociological imagination enhances mine).

The Rev. Canon Dan Webster, aka, my husband, deserves special kudos and not just because of his emotional and spiritual generosity. Dan has always understood—and implored church leadership to understand—the value of church communications ministry. I am the grateful beneficiary of his fervent support for those of us called to this ministry as well as his personal commitment to preach and live the Gospel message of love and justice.

When it comes to digital communications, the future is already here—in the secular world. In the world of church? Not so much, which is why I'm especially indebted to Trish Vanni for inviting me to write this book, helping me think it through, and then shepherding the approval process. For his responsiveness, enthusiasm for the subject, and terrific sense of humor, I thank Andy Edwards, managing editor. Thanks and praise to the production team that included Stephanie Lancour, Stefan Killen, Julie Surma, and Shirley Richardson.

Always and forever, thanks be to God.

SECTION I

FRAMEWORKS FOR UNDERSTANDING

Chapter 1   Defining Social Media

Thanks in part to its still-evolving nature, you'll find quite a few definitions of social media floating around cyberspace. Don't be at all surprised if you get confused while searching for one that makes sense to you. You're likely to encounter lots of technical jargon, mostly from business and industry, which, let's be honest, tends to make church folk nervous. The sectors and the jargon.

As for me and my software, we serve the Lord by keeping tech-talk and jargon to a minimum (see Chapter 23: Jargon Alert). And so it has come to pass that I've managed to develop a relatively simple and accessible definition of social media.

Like other early adopters,[1] my definition of social media has evolved over the years. It has changed as social media has changed. It has changed as my understanding of community and church has been transformed by using it. Here's my current common language definition of social media:

> *Social media are web-based tools for interaction that, in addition to conversation, allow users to share content such as photos, videos, and links to resources.*

Hopefully you won't have to read my definition more than twice to understand social media are *digital tools* for sharing conversation and content. Please do return to this definition when more complicated ones threaten your comprehension. Or sanity. Here, for example, is a social media definition that always triggers a slight case of aphasia in tech-literate me:

Social media are digital platforms used for engagement
and content delivery.

What might help you crack the code of complex, jargon-laden definitions of social media is knowing that these key terms can be and often are used interchangeably—sometimes in the same brain-scrambling sentence:

web-based = *online* and *digital*
tools = *platforms* and *digital technologies*
interaction = *engagement*

(Confession: I do tend to use the word "engagement" when I mean "interaction" or "involvement." Forgive me my jargon trespasses.)

Moving right along.

You'll find definitions that emphasize how to use social media tools for managing and monitoring the public perception of brand identity. These definitions will make more sense in the context of church if you think in terms of *mission*:

Social media tools can be used to manage and monitor
public perception of your congregation's mission.

Untangling the World Wide Web	
	Online digital as a medium for . . .
Web 1.0	broadcast with static, read-only content (e.g., websites, e-newsletters).
Web 2.0	interaction and engagement with use-generated content (e.g., social networking tools).
Web 3.0	portable personalized content and search functions (e.g., mobile websites, smartphone apps).

Definitions of social media tend to become murky when out-come (e.g., social action) is confused with means (e.g., tools).

Over the years, I've noticed this happening when social media is characterized as a culture in and of itself rather than a set of technological tools for catalyzing shifts in attitudes and beliefs. Attitudes and beliefs are core aspects of culture that can, when shifted, lead to social action.

Here, I'm thinking about the role Twitter played during the Iraqi election in March 2010 and the Arab Spring in November 2011, and, as I'm writing, in shifting public opinion about gun control in the aftermath of the Newtown, Connecticut, school shooting in December 2012.

It's easy to get caught up in relatively esoteric conversations about living, working, and ministering within a "social media" or "digital" culture. You'll find these discussions unfolding mostly on blogs and e-zines where there's more space for narrative, but also in brief bursts of conversation on Twitter among those who have been using (or observing) social media for a few years.

These conversations appeal to those of us who delight in epistemological romps. Plus, there's no denying that we now live in a social media culture. Social media has, for example, completely transformed the way we understand the cultural

---

Three Conceptual Barriers to Social Media Success

Although we're rapidly approaching the tipping point for so-cial media acceptance, there are still many people in active min-istry who cling to these false ideas, believing that social media:

- isn't real, therefore nothing generated with or from it is authentic;
- undermines church-the-building, therefore cannot be used to inspire attendance or participation; or
- should be considered a nonessential luxury because it takes too much time to learn and use.

construct known as privacy (see box: "Nothing Is Concealed . . ." on p. 103). Cultural perceptions of time and timing have also been changed by social media (see box: Life Cycle of a Virtual Community, p. 28). These days everything seems more immediate and faster, even for those who reject online technology. This, in turn, has changed culture-based expectations about what constitutes availability and responsiveness.[2]

Social media has forever changed what it means to participate. Seriously, did you ever imagine network television stations would invite viewers to join real-time online conversations about prime-time shows and news events? Welcome to the global living room and worldwide peanut gallery—social media culture!

Still, as you get started, I urge you to focus on first understanding why and how to use social media tools *before* diving into meta-level conversations at the intersection of social science and theology. Join these conversations *after* mastering the basics because social media, in some form, is here to stay. And, trust me on this, you'll need to get comfy with Web 2.0 pretty quickly. Mobile communication tools (Web 3.0) are already here, stimulating another transformation in digital ministry, which I define as using digital tools for ministry as well as ministering to those who fear social media.

THOUGHT BYTES

Whether you're just now getting started with social media or have been using it for a while, begin at the beginning and ask:

- For which of the terms most commonly used to define social media do we need more clarification?
- How does defining social media help us?
- What are the practical consequences of moving forward without defining what we mean by social media?

Chapter 2 Thinking Theologically

You'll need to develop the habit of consciously thinking about social media within a basic theological framework if you want to build church and deepen faith with these tools. Simply put, you'll need to know what you believe about God, as well as what you believe about God's ongoing, eternal communication with us. If you're blessed to be in charge of using social media for a church community, you'll also need to know how your denomination might specifically interpret and articulate Christian doctrine.

Where to begin? That's the easy part.

This opening passage from the Gospel of John is cited by everyone involved with church communication: "In the beginning was the Word, and the Word was with God, and the Word was God" (John 1:1).[3] We start with this verse because it captures what we believe about the radical power of communication, namely, that God has spoken all creation into being and continues to speak to and through us.

More advanced theological conversations, like ones about whether virtual community is or can be incarnational, are grounded in this verse as John's gospel narrative continues: "And the Word became flesh and lived among us, and we have seen his glory, the glory as of a father's only son, full of grace and truth" (John 1:14).[4]

But unless this level of inquiry calls to you, you do not need to dive into the work about digital ministry and incarnationality—certainly not before learning *why* to use social media and how each platform works.

In the beginning, your theological framework needs, at minimum, to be grounded in knowing that Christians embrace the following beliefs, some of which you'll recognize from the creeds we recite during worship.

We believe in:

- one God whose grace and mercy was revealed through the birth, life, death, and resurrection of Jesus;
- the Holy Spirit, who has spoken through prophets and continues communicating God's wisdom and guidance;
- God-inspired Scripture that communicates ethical standards and guidelines for behavior;
- actively living Gospel teachings about love, service, faith, and hope as individuals and within a community of believers;
- sacraments instituted by Jesus as visible signs of inward grace. Note: we all agree that baptism and Communion are sacraments instituted by Jesus. Whether

Christ Has No Online Presence but Yours

In 2010, I created this contemporary take on Saint Teresa of Avila's well-known prayer "Christ Has No Body." Since then, my version has shown up in a variety of places on the internet. Someone once contacted me for permission about setting it to music.[5] For your contemplative pleasure:

> Christ has no online presence but yours,
> No blog, no Facebook page but yours,
> Yours are the tweets through which love touches this world,
> Yours are the posts through which the Gospel is shared,
> Yours are the updates through which hope is revealed.
> Christ has no online presence but yours,
> No blog, no Facebook page but yours.

confirmation, reconciliation, marriage, holy orders, and anointing of the sick are viewed as sacraments depends on the denomination.

What we believe shapes how we relate to one another and interact with the world—wherever and however we relate and interact. You don't have to make too great a leap of faith or

Virtual Sacraments? Not Really

Hang out in and around virtual communities long enough and you'll encounter debates about whether sacraments can "work" online. In this instance the word "work" is synonymous with "valid" in the liturgical sense.

Plug the words "virtual Eucharist" into Google and you'll find links to posts on this topic from 2009. Back then, the issue emerged relative to what was happening at the Anglican Cathedral in Second Life.[6]

The suggestion that we ought to develop a theology of virtual sacraments as valid within that context was shot down in a flurry of well-reasoned posts by liturgists. (If you do check this out, be sure to read what New Zealand-based Anglican priest Rev. Bosco Peters wrote about the tension between virtual and so-called real worlds.)

Next, plug the words "virtual confession" into Google and you'll see the conversation flaring up again in 2011 when "Confession: A Roman Catholic App" was created for the iPhone. If it ever was approved by the Vatican as first reported, that approval was swiftly yanked.

Your great take-away from these conversations should be that everyone seems to agree that digital technology provides ways to *prepare* for sacraments, not receive them. Confusing sacramental preparation or online participation (e.g., attending and tweeting a live-streamed wedding or baptism) with receiving a sacrament is counterproductive. Don't do that! Begging you.

intellect to understand that by extension, what we believe provides a framework for using social media.

Now add what we know about Jesus as communicator.

Every gospel reminds us about how Jesus actively engaged with disciples and detractors. He used conversations, storytelling, inquiry, debate, dialogue, and truth-telling to challenge then-prevailing notions about God, faith, ethics, relationships, and religious business-as-usual. From the gospels we learn

'Tis a Gift to Be Gifted

Everyone is graced with spiritual gifts. We believe our prayers to receive the ones we want but don't yet have are welcomed (1 Cor 12:1-11). Different gifts are associated with each church ministry. Clearly everyone is better off if those involved with coffee hour have the gift of hospitality rather than the wisdom gifts, although I'm open to being wrong about that.

When it comes to communication ministry, the spiritual gifts of faith, being able to convey the Gospel, encouraging and welcoming others, and being able to lead are essential. This is equally true for digital ministry.

Secular skills are also necessary. For these you may pray without ceasing, but getting hands-on training is probably a smarter choice for faster results.

For digital ministry you'll need to learn how computer technology (hardware and software) works and what to do when it doesn't; editorial and graphic skills specifically for online content; how to formulate a communication strategy in general; and how to integrate online tools that include but are not limited to social media. You'll also need to learn how to organize and manage a project, including when to delegate or outsource tasks to skilled others.

And here's the Good News of digital ministry these days: You do not need to know HTML or how to write computer code. Content Management Systems (CMS) have delivered the non-geeks among us from ever having to do that.

about where Jesus preached and how he commissioned followers to spread the astonishingly good news about being loved by
God and extending that love to others, for a change.

That was then.

These days, like the saints before us, we're invited to go forth
and do likewise. Online tools provide us with the means to teach
with a previously unimaginable reach. Today's mission field is
online, so thinking theologically helps us use social media to
reach out while staying in alignment with the faith we profess.

Here's how our faith provides a framework for using social
media:

- Believing in a gracious and merciful God calls us to
  be gracious and merciful during online interactions in
  terms of content and tone.
- Believing in the power of the Holy Spirit inspires us to
  be open to whatever is revealed during online conversations about God's presence and our choices relative
  to faith and religious expressions thereof.
- Believing that Scripture provides a foundation for ethical
  living calls us to use social media as yet another tool
  to convey Scripture, not only by broadcasting verses
  but also by providing opportunities for their study and
  discussion.
- Believing in Gospel teachings calls us to model what
  we believe while using social media by offering helpful information, providing comfort, sharing joy, and
  engaging in conversations that build and unite, rather
  than tear down or divide the people of God.
- Believing in the grace available through sacraments
  calls us to encourage their receipt, support preparation
  for them, and invite others to witness their celebration.

Wait, there's more!

Christianity is a religion anchored in community. Jesus set
the standard by declaring God present when two or three are

gathered (Matt 18:20). And I cannot resist pointing out how Jesus was calling us friends long before Facebook "friending" was invented.

The church always was and remains an assembly of believers. At least two centuries would pass after Jesus' crucifixion and resurrection as Christ before "the church" became a building. Both biblically and historically we know that early followers of Jesus as Christ, committed to the Way, met in private homes.

The cloud of witnesses takes on new meaning as we use social media to live out our baptismal call. Today, people gather online. Social media provides a means for sharing faith as well as modeling Christian life beyond the building we call church.

We already have a theological framework that provides everything we need to justify using social media as a tool for ministry. Thinking theologically—seeing social media through the God-lens—will help you use it to share abundantly the joys and challenges of a life in Christ.[7]

THOUGHT BYTES

Take another look at the Nicene Creed, reread the Synoptic Gospels (i.e., Matthew, Mark, Luke), and ask:

- How does viewing social media through a God-lens help us understand social media as a tool for sharing the Gospel message and conduit for the Holy Spirit?
- What do we need to understand about community in general and Christian community in particular before using social media?
- When should we be cautious about using social media as a tool for evangelism?

Chapter 3   Thinking Generationally

These days nearly all churches throughout North America face the reality of needing to attract and keep congregants. While social media is proving to be a great tool for evangelism, anyone using it to build church faces the dicey challenge of reaching out to younger congregants without ignoring or alienating the older stalwart faithful.

You can prevent this challenge from flaring up into a major problem by learning more about how age groups are distributed into generations and the characteristics of these cohorts. Get ready for a crash course in demographics.

Like sex, race, ethnicity, and socioeconomic status,[8] age is a primary characteristic that social scientists (i.e., anthropologists, demographers, economists, political scientists, and sociologists) and market researchers invoke to explain social (i.e., group) behavior.

Generations are always defined by birth year, which identifies when members have made the transition from childhood to adulthood. Focusing on birth year makes it easier to zoom in on the major cultural, social, political, economic, and technological events that have shaped the attitudes, beliefs, and behaviors of that generation.

For example, cohorts growing up during the rapid continuous development of digital technologies and online communications are more likely to swiftly embrace social media tools and all iterations. In contrast, generations for which technology has changed more slowly, albeit more radically during the twentieth century, tend to be whimperingly weary of yet more change.

These, by the way, are the folks who reject hardware as well as software, proudly declaring themselves Luddites, a reference to nineteenth-century artisans who protested the Industrial Revolution by smashing manufacturing equipment. And wasn't that just so effective? Not really.

To date, these cohorts have been clearly defined and named: Silent Generation (aka, GI Generation), Baby Boomers, Generation X (aka, GenXers), and Millennials (aka, Digital Natives). (See box: Talking about Whose Generation?, p. 14.)[9]

By now these cohort monikers are so commonly used that you probably have no trouble conjuring up assumptions whenever you see or hear them referenced. Thanks to the work of social scientists, we now know enough to make these general observations about each cohort and its communication preferences:[10]

- *Silent Generation:* practical, dedicated, patient, and willing to delay gratification; tend to prefer direct communication via traditional media.
- *Boomers:* optimistic, driven, competitive, involved, and committed to personal growth; tend to prefer in-person communication as well as reading online and in print.
- *GenXers:* skeptical, outcome-focused, committed to diversity, self-reliant, globally aware, and technoliter-

Talking about Whose Generation?	
Cohort	**Birth Years (by 2013)**
Silent Generation	1925–45 (68–88)
Baby Boomers	1946–64 (49–67)
Generation X	1965–81 (32–48)
Millennials*	1982–95 (18–31)

* Also known as "Digital Natives."

ate; tend to prefer direct, immediate, and interactive communication using online tools.

- *Millennials/Digital Natives:* optimistic, confident, ambitious, impatient, civic-minded, highly collaborative, committed to diversity and inclusivity in relationships, and technoliterate; prefer social media and texting.

When it comes to understanding why and when social media tools work, I've come to believe that age has more explanatory value than sex and possibly as much significance as socioeconomic status (see Chapter 11: Bridging the Digital Divide). For what it's worth, this is major because I've spent decades using sex, gender, and class to explain . . . everything.

So what to do with well-documented insights about age cohorts? For one thing, thinking generationally can help you understand why some cohorts will prefer some social media tools and reject others. For even more illumination, factor in how each cohort learned basic literacy.

For example, members of the Silent Generation and Baby Boomers are more likely to prefer blogs because this social media tool involves reading and writing. The passion GenXers

Generations & Social Media Tools				
	Silent Generation	*Baby Boomers*	*Generation X*	*Millennials (Digital Natives)*
Blogs	✓	✓	✓	
Facebook	✓	✓	✓	
Instagram/ Pinterest		✓	✓	✓
Twitter			✓	✓
YouTube/Vimeo		✓	✓	✓

and Millennials have for YouTube, Pinterest, and Instagram makes sense once you know about how curricula shifted to emphasize oral, aural, and visual learning when those cohorts attended elementary school (see Chapter 4: Learning Styles).

You'll want to get into the habit of thinking generationally because doing so will help you choose social media tools more strategically.

Social media tools only work if the right ones are chosen and intelligently combined with more traditional forms of communication (see Chapter 10: Print Is Not Dead; It's Being Transfigured). What's the distribution of age cohorts in your existing congregation? Which generation(s) do you hope to reach? Social media may be as alienating for Silent Generation congregants as printed newsletters are for GenXers and Millennials.

Learning more about generational values and attitudes can help identify points of convergence between cohorts. Review the characteristics listed above and get ready for a shocker: Boomers and Millennials share some key attitudes. How might you use your new awareness to bridge generation gaps?

Even more important for building church and faith, consider how thinking generationally could help you foster an environment of mutual regard and abiding mercy whenever you minister to others—with or without social media.

THOUGHT BYTES

To get the most out of thinking generationally relative to social media, ask:

- What do we know about the age composition of our church community?
- How accurate are the assumptions we make about attitudes, beliefs, and behaviors within age cohorts?
- Are we willing and able to gather more information about the age composition of our church community and those we want to reach?

Chapter 4   Learning Styles

Have you noticed how, even though Jesus is most often de-
picted teaching with people gathered closely around him, our
older traditional church sanctuaries are set up classroom-style?
Pulpit at the front. Pews or chairs lined up and facing forward in
rows. Very tidy but not optimal for either hearing or listening;
more conducive to viewing rather than seeing. At least we get to
touch bread and wine. Sometimes. Given what we know about
how people learn, it's truly a miracle anything ever sinks into
minds and hearts at church.

Knowing about and embracing the Visual-Auditory-Kinesthetic
(VAK) model of learning will make a major difference in how you
use digital as well as traditional communication tools to build
church and faith.

The VAK model, developed during the 1920s by teaching spe-
cialists, became widely used by educators and trainers by the
1990s. It's an accepted, long-standing model because it accu-
rately captures the fact that learning is not a one-size-fits-all
process. Each of us has a learning style that's primarily but not
exclusively visual, auditory, or kinesthetic. Most people have a
blend of at least two styles that shape how and how well we
will learn.

Primary and secondary school teachers routinely study the
VAK model as well as methods for using it to enhance student
comprehension. Curriculum developers use it to create instructional materials. Indeed, chances for learning content are slightly
better for students attending sacramental preparation and reli-

gious formation classes because most of those materials are developed by educators who understand the importance of accommodating all learning styles.

No matter how you're called to serve the people of God, knowing more about the VAK model will help you minister. If nothing else, it will help you better understand how people participate in church and hopefully shift your judgments about their seemingly odd or rude behavior.

Congregants who read during worship are more visual than auditory. Those who seem to be doodling on the worship bulletin or texting from smartphones are kinesthetic learners. I know this because I'm a visual-kinesthetic learner and fiddling around helps whatever is being proclaimed from the pulpit sink into my brain mush. If I'm ever invited to visit your church, feel free to knit a prayer shawl or post tweets while I'm talking; I won't be offended.

The VAK model reframes what might seem like inattentive or overly dramatic behavior into appropriate and possibly necessary ways to join in worship. Congregants and pew-mates who lip-sync liturgy and come to life during hymns are more auditory, as are those who seem to become more present during Communion upon hearing "the body of Christ." People who seem to receive

Learning Styles & Social Media Tools			
	Visual seeing/ reading	*Auditory* listening/ speaking	*Kinesthetic* touching/ doing
Blogs	✓		
Facebook	✓		
Instagram/Pinterest	✓		
Twitter	✓		✓
YouTube/Vimeo		✓	

more deeply when consecrated bread is pressed into their hands are kinesthetic. Worship committee members who insist the sanctuary be festooned with liturgically correct banners are visually oriented. The ones who insist on liturgical dance and clap in rhythm during hymns are predominantly kinesthetic.

Please consider that what might be massively annoying to you is helping someone else become part of community worship. Instead of shooting them looks that might kill without a promise of resurrection, simply move to another seat in the sanctuary. If you're the pastor, consider how allowing the use of ringer-silenced smartphones in church might support congregants whose comprehension is otherwise limited by traditional structures of worship and preaching.

Learning styles also help explain why some church communication tools work only some of the time and with only some of the people.

Social media tools like blogs, which allow embedded media, make it possible to reach out to visual as well as auditory or kinesthetic learners. Others, like Pinterest and YouTube, do not have as wide a reach. For example, I love Twitter because it involves typing short sentences (i.e., a kinesthetic activity) into an easy-to-see real-time message box (i.e., a visual element).

Appreciating learning styles will help you understand how a social media tool that's welcomed as blessedly easy by one person could be cursed as impossibly difficult by another.

Last but not least, the VAK model will help you determine how to distribute content and conversation into whichever social media tools you eventually choose (see Section II: Choosing Social Media). Choosing the right mix of social media tools will, in turn, make it possible for people of faith within and beyond your sanctuary to build community and Christ's universal church.

THOUGHT BYTES

As you add learning styles to your way of understanding people's behavior, ask:

- What will help us use the VAK learning style model to most effectively choose social media tools?
- How could we use the VAK learning style model to educate church leaders and congregants about the value of allowing (silenced) smartphone use in the church sanctuary?
- Are we clear about how our own learning styles might be impeding our comfort with digital ministry?

Personality Types

Of all the fear-based concerns about social media issuing forth from mouths of naysayers, the one about it being alienating and isolating distresses me the most. Using social media has had the exact opposite effect on my own life and I know this to be true for many others.

Thanks to social media and what some might view as an overabundance of hardware—two monitors, a laptop, a netbook, and a smartphone—I now delight in sharing prayers, laughs, and culture commentary as well as news with a far-flung group of friends and colleagues. Many have become very dear; most I have never met in person.

Daily, hourly, and minute-by-minute if I so choose, I can discover who is serving the Lord with gladness, who is praying that sorrow will indeed give way to joy in the morning, who is celebrating the sacraments, who is fretting about writing a sermon, who is seeking God in all things, who is drinking way too much coffee, who needs a nap.

Left to my own devices and in the absence of internet access, I'd happily wander through days and nights without interacting with another human being. Social media has changed all that.

Even after years of active use, I remain amazed at how social media has helped me become more, not less, connected to people, groups, and organizations. To use a much-loved concept from Ignatian spirituality, thanks to social media I've become much more of a person for others, a more willing witness to life

Myers-Briggs Type Indicator® Cheat Sheet

Anchored in Carl Jung's theory of personality, the Myers-Briggs Type Indicator (MBTI®) is a rigorous, time-tested way to assess personality type worth exploring in more detail, especially since it seems to be the *lingua franca* for clergy. The Myers & Briggs Foundation (www.myersbriggs.org) is a good place to start, but here's a brief summary.

An MBTI assessment yields a four-letter typology representing how individuals draw upon functions within these four basic dichotomies:

1. Extraversion (E)/Introversion (I)
2. Sensing (S)/Intuition (N)
3. Thinking (T)/Feeling (F)
4. Judging (J)/Perception (P)

The four-letter MBTI-type formula uses the letters E, I, S, N, T, F, J, and P to reveal mental functioning preferences in order of dominance. These mental functions work synergistically to reveal personality and explain behavior.

There are sixteen possible combinations, and this dynamic approach to personality typology recognizes that preferences may shift during the life cycle. Note: The MBTI measures preferences, not abilities. Someone might be completely able to manage group settings but hope to Almighty God they won't have to.

While this surface-level information won't make you an instant expert, it should help you digest MBTI alphabet soup when it's served.

as it unfolds. I've become more willing to reach out when I'm in spiritual and secular need. How could this be?

Mystery solved by turning to psychology, the social science devoted to studying human behavior and mental processes (e.g., thoughts, feelings, motives). More specifically, the answer to why social media invites people like me into vibrant community involvement is revealed by studying the personality theory developed by twentieth-century psychoanalyst Carl Jung and its practical manifestation in the Myers-Briggs Type Indicator (MBTI). (See box: Myers-Briggs Type Indicator Cheat Sheet, p. 23.)

Jung came up with the term we use to describe those who much prefer solitude over crowds, silence over sound, and written exchanges to verbal interactions. We're known as introverts and we tend to love social media because it makes it easier for us to sustain relationships.

Rules Made to Be Noticed

Among the oh-so-many rules cobbled together by social analysts, here are two that will come in handy as you use social media:

80/20 Rule (Pareto's principle): For most events, 80 percent of the effects come from 20 percent of the causes. Use this rule to make sure that 80 percent of your social media content will generate community-building engagement (e.g., blog comments, Facebook/Twitter conversations).

Limit broadcasting (i.e., reporting news, promoting events) to 20 percent of your social media content. Put that stuff into e-newsletters and on your website, remembering, of course, to remove it when it's no longer news.

90/9/1 Rule (Coined by Jakob Nielsen):[11] Within most online communities, 90 percent observe and neither contribute nor participate, 9 percent of community members will participate or contribute occasionally, and 1 percent dominate the community by providing almost all content and conversation.

Use this rule to understand that you're reaching many more people than are letting on, individuals who may in fact consider themselves part of your community. You also want to use it to acknowledge and appreciate the 1 percent. They're your evangelists and ambassadors.

You'd think it would be the other way around since the successful use of social media requires consistent, ongoing interaction, right? It's not.

Although gregarious extroverts appreciate the value of social media, they always prefer face-to-face interactions. Extroverts are energized by groups, unfazed by boisterous conversations with high-velocity cross talk; the more the merrier—in person. Check it out and you'll discover that extroverts are the ones who worry about social media becoming a replacement for, rather than a way to enhance, existing relationships or forging new ones.

Not so for introverts, especially those with intuitive and feeling tendencies. We're sensitive souls and here's news you can use: many of us look and act a whole lot tougher than we are! Social media is a blessing, making it easier for us to engage in the consistent, ongoing interaction generally required for full membership in a community.

When asked about its benefits, self-identified INFP (Introvert, Intuitive, Feeling, Perceptive) and INFJ (Introvert, Intuitive, Feeling, Judging) types typically say that social media:[12]

- helps me connect with people I'd probably not talk to in a public space because I dislike crowds/groups;
- makes it possible to interact with lots of people in a way that does not drain me;
- gives the opportunity to meet someone before meeting in person, which helps me connect more easily once we meet IRL (in real life);
- allows me to observe when I want and take action when I get enough courage to do so;
- enables me to extend a conversation I might not risk face-to-face;
- allows me to respond at my own pace without putting me on the spot.

Introverts also note how being able to sort friends and followers into lists, a function provided by all major social media platforms, makes it easier to filter input and reduce the over-stimulation that typically agitates and may frighten shy people.

Every church has members who are often perceived as aloof flakes because they won't stay for coffee hour, they register but don't show up for events, or they preview tickets for the rummage sale not because they want great deals but because they can't tolerate crowds. Time to reframe those perceptions. These congregants are probably introverts who just might emerge from isolation to become valued members of your community if you provide opportunities to do so through social media.

THOUGHT BYTES

Knowing that personality type is a factor that helps explain people's comfort with and willingness to use social media, ask:

- Do we know enough about our own personality to understand why we like or reject certain types of social media?
- How might we choose and use social media tools to accommodate personality types?
- What can we do to alleviate concerns people might have about social media being alienating and isolating?

Chapter 6   Virtual Community Is Real Community

Social media has opened up yet another portal for seeing and being seen, for knowing and being known, for being in and belonging to community.

Some communities are extensions of already existing physical communities. Others are completely virtual—created, gathered, developed, and sustained exclusively online. Still others are communities where the boundaries between what is "real" (i.e., physical) and what is "virtual" (i.e., online) are permeable (see chart: The Trajectory of Engagement, p. 29).

When social media was first developed and everyone got a glimmer about how it might be used, distinctions between real and virtual worlds were helpful. Not anymore. Turns out virtual community is real community. This is also true for the world of being and doing church online. Just ask anyone who has invested enough time in online conversations about faith, spirituality, religion, and church to discover the ever-expanding universe of support available within and beyond denominations.

Online communities of faith are real to members who have come to rely on them for inspiration and support.

Don't be scared off by my mention of time and energy. In fact, you've already invested time and energy, or are willing to do so whenever you join *any* physical community. Time and energy put into quality interaction is what makes a group of individuals who share interests and concerns become a community no matter where it's located.

True communities—ones whose members stay connected and are mutually supportive—flow from interactions over a period of time. In the physical world, these periods of time are long in duration even for church folks, despite our hope that Christian community will form more swiftly because of shared beliefs.

Take a moment to recall a time when you started attending a church that was new to you.

How many times did you exchange a sign of peace with strangers before chatting with them after worship? How many conversations did it take before you exchanged personal contact

Life Cycle of a Virtual Community

I move quickly—in a prayerful discernment way, of course—but even so, I'm routinely blown away by how quickly virtual communities form, grow, decline, and eventually leave this mortal online coil.

Without any scientifically rigorous evidence but years of participant observation and experience as an online community manager to back me up, I've come to believe that virtual time moves three times faster. In most instances. By this I mean that one month or year of engagement via social media seems equal to three months or years in the world of physical community.

Practically speaking, an online community can, in one year, cycle through everything it takes three years for a physical community to develop or accomplish.

Leadership can emerge within one month rather than three, cliques within three months rather than six. Unless new leadership emerges and long-time participants become willing to serve as elders to welcome newcomers, an online community can become moribund in fewer than three years.

Whenever you use social media, remembering the comparative speed with which everything happens should help you create realistic timelines, manage expectations, celebrate accomplishments, let go with satisfaction, and move on without regret to create something new.

information? How long did it take for you to then use that information to reach out? How long before anyone used it to invite you to participate in anything?

If your experience has been anything like mine, it took quite a while to shift from exchanging pleasantries in the narthex to considering other congregants as friends. If you're an introvert, it could have taken years.[13]

The process by which individuals form groups that eventually coalesce into communities is the same online and off. Social media simply shifts time-tested principles of community

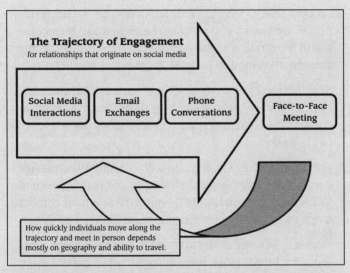

The Trajectory of Engagement
for relationships that originate on social media

Social Media Interactions → Email Exchanges → Phone Conversations → Face-to-Face Meeting

How quickly individuals move along the trajectory and meet in person depends mostly on geography and ability to travel.

Social media tends to connect rather than isolate users. Relationships starting as conversations via social media frequently lead to in-person meetings as geography and time allow. Email exchanges and phone conversations usually, but not always, pave the way to meeting IRL (in real life).

Do not assume that whatever begins on social media stays on social media. Now that social media has become a normative tool for communication, it's common for individuals who first meet in a physical environment (e.g., church) to "friend" and "follow" each other to continue the conversation via social media.

development to a more fluid, broader, and faster moving environment. Maybe *that* is what's scary? If so, I understand; now repeat after me: *Veni Sancte Spiritus.*

My prayer is that eliminating unnecessary distinctions and counting it all real will make it easier for you to use social media to build community. After all, you already know how church communities and ministries work, when and why they don't or can't. Social media simply speeds up the rate at which the following occurs:

> *Leadership and rules for conduct emerge.* When, why, and how does that usually happen? What do being present and accountability look like? You cannot wander in and mostly out of community and expect to be viewed as a member—not in the physical world and not online, although online communities tend to be more forgiving of wanderers.

> *Special interest groups or cliques develop.* What determines whether these are benign or destructive? How do communities and ministries typically handle small groups or cliques?

> *Conflict threatens stability.* How do communities manage conflict? Are management strategies and techniques tied to the type of community or ministry in which conflict crops up? (See Chapter 25: Managing Online Conflict.)

> *Members become bored and restless.* How do ministries remain vibrant? How does change tend to bubble up to the surface? When is it time to disband an existing community or ministry?

Simply apply what you already know. That's it! Simple and easier than you might think as you get started with social media. Just remember that whatever occurs in so-called real community will happen in virtual community. It's *all* real, especially for those whose online experiences have led to more enthusiastic church attendance and a more expansive vision of Christian community.

THOUGHT BYTES

To open up new avenues for being and doing church with social media, ask:

- What becomes possible once we accept the principle that virtual community is real community?
- What do we already know about our community that will help us use social media tools to continue building and growing?
- What sorts of additional or different community-building skills might be required to extend our community into an online environment?

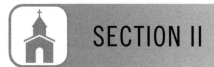

SECTION II

CHOOSING SOCIAL MEDIA

Chapter 7   Strategic Planning

Until very recently, when worship attendance started declining for just about every Christian denomination, church leadership didn't have to think strategically about much of anything except maybe fund-raising and overflow seating for the annual Christmas pageant. People of faith attended church regularly and stayed loyal to the religious tradition of their youth.

Today this is no longer automatically the case for a variety of reasons. Most significant, perhaps, is the sharp increase in how many people currently self-identify as "spiritual but not religious." They have been termed the "Nones" by The Pew Forum on Religion & Public Life and have been causing much weeping and gnashing of teeth among ministers.[14]

Strategic planning, once viewed with suspicion as a secular business process, is now being adapted for church use, albeit not as frequently as it probably should be for communication ministry. While it always helps to invoke the Holy Spirit, effectively communicating church and faith doesn't miraculously happen. It requires careful planning. This is especially true when choosing and using social media tools.

While all social media platforms engage users in similar ways, each will appeal to a slightly different audience. Finding a good fit for your ministry involves thinking strategically and then making strategic choices (see Appendix A: Strategic Choices, p. 113).

"We need to use social media because everyone else uses it" is not a strategy. Social media in and of itself is not a strategy.

Social media is a tool that must be selected and used with purposeful forethought. There's no getting around this if you ever hope to get specific messages to specific audiences to inspire specific actions to generate specific results.

But how on earth can you create a plan for using tools whose function you don't understand? You can't. This is why I always recommend futzing with personal accounts before setting anything up for your church or organization. Get familiar with each of the dominant social media platforms; discover how they work and if you like using them. Please do this important pre-work and wrestle with these core issues before setting up institutional accounts:

> *What do we want to happen as a result of using these tools?* While engagement (i.e., interaction) is evidence of social media success, you'll need to clearly define the actions and behaviors you want to emerge because congregants are engaging with you and one another via social media. Are your goals realistic?

> *Who do we most want to reach?* Remember to get information about how your audience receives and absorbs information. You probably want to reach more than one group of people, so who, in order of importance, are your intended audiences?

> *How will we know we've succeeded?* Remember that although these tools speed up communication and make it possible for groups to form quickly, building community always takes longer than anyone expects. How will you respond if your parish council, vestry, church board, or some other group with authority asks if social media is working?

Don't rush this process. But don't go too far the other way, turning it into an extended inquiry by a committee of well-meaning but unqualified participants.

Create a detailed, actionable plan that's written out rather than housed in someone's imagination. Next, get it reviewed and approved by someone with hands-on experience with social media as well as marketing communications. Thankfully, it's no longer all that difficult to find people who use social media to build church and faith. (Helpful hint: We're online!) All this should happen *before* choosing and using social media for ministry.

What's that? You've already taken the plunge and set up a Twitter account, Facebook page, and Pinterest boards? Unless you've already generated a thriving community, I urge you to consider suspending all but basic activity on your accounts until assessing if, in fact, you've chosen the right ones. But don't just disappear from cyberspace. Do let friends, followers, and blog

---

Holy Great Expectations

When used wisely and well, social media can help your church:

- build Christian community within and beyond church-the-building;
- celebrate the sacraments;
- deliver time-sensitive news and information;
- educate newcomers about your church community;
- enhance the website's functionality;
- establish and maintain a local, regional, or national presence;
- gather feedback from congregants;
- minister to the homebound and those unable to attend;
- organize, publicize, and invite people to events;
- preach the Gospel;
- model Gospel values and Christian love;
- provide a safe, secure place to gather for online fellowship; and
- share stories to deepen faith and inspire action.

readers know you're rethinking your social media presence. While you're at it, ask for suggestions. No response? No problem. You've just collected useful data about how your current strategy isn't working.

Commit to doing the necessary work of strategic planning and you'll be well equipped to choose one or more social media platforms to meet your communication and community-building needs.

If you're worried about generating anxiety by bandying about the words "strategic planning," then tell everyone you're prayerfully discerning how to choose social media tools for the kingdom, the power, and the glory of God, forever and ever, world without end.

THOUGHT BYTES

Developing a strategy for choosing and tactics for using social media tools should happen before setting up any accounts and shouldn't be ignored if accounts already exist. To manage resistance to strategic planning, ask:

- Which factors or concerns are causing resistance to planning our social media usage?
- Are we willing to risk failure by setting up or continuing to manage social media accounts without a plan?
- What could we do to overcome resistance and move forward with a planning process?

Chapter 8   Participants and Participation

Before laying any claim to creating a complete and actionable strategy for social media, you'll need to know lots about your hoped-for audience. You'll need to collect (or find) demographic information about them (see Section I: Frameworks for Understanding). You'll also need to know how they already use or are most likely to use social media. Do they participate? If so, how? By observing, joining conversations, or simply putting a user profile up on one of the better-known platforms? Do they offer information (i.e., content) to help others or almost always post links to their own work?

When it comes to participants and participation, lots of great conceptual work has already been done, primarily for business and industry. It's work that can be easily adapted for use by church . . . if everyone agrees not to freak out about terms like "consumer" or "target audience" or "brand."[15]

I, for one, do not waste time freaking out about this because every organizational world has its own jargon. I simply replace biz-speak with church-speak to imagine how business intelligence might apply to church and faith communities.

Depending on the situation, I replace the words "target audience" or "consumer" with "church" or "congregants" or "ministers" or "church leadership." Not a problem. Nor do I fret about creating typologies. I'm a sociologist, so sorting people into groups depending on behavior is positively thrilling for me. And useful.

When it comes to typologies of social media participants and participation, I remain unwaveringly keen on the Social Technographics Ladder developed by Forrester analysts Charlene Li and Josh Bernoff. They coined the term "social technographics" to describe their classification of people based on how social technologies get used and chose a ladder to represent increasing levels of participation.[16]

Since 2007, their typology has helped communication strategists think in more accurate categories about how people use social media, which is something well worth learning about before deciding which platforms to launch or which existing ones to punt.

Their first Social Technographics Ladder had six rungs. Inactives, those who don't bother with social media, were at the lowest rung. At the top? Creators who actively participate on social media by publishing or uploading original content. In between, in order of increased participation: Spectators, Joiners, Collectors, and Critics.

I immediately sought to locate myself on the ladder and was soon stumbling up and down the thing, splayed out in every fabulously self-explanatory category but Inactive. I am anything but Inactive on social media.

In 2010, a rung for Conversationalists was added to acknowledge what was happening on Twitter and Facebook, platforms with exponential growth.[17] By then, Twitter had finally become notable for generating conversation among followers, and status updates on Facebook were clearly stimulating more engagement among friends.

Perhaps rungs will be added as social media participation becomes more nuanced with use over time. A few faithful members of the weekly church social media (#chsocm) chat on Twitter have twondered why the ladder didn't include Curators and Connectors.[18] But with or without further enhancements, the Social Technographics Ladder provides a practical way to think about communicating church and faith with social media.

Take another look at your audience and think about where they might be on this ladder. Where do you want them to be?

Locating your audience(s) will help you choose tools that, in addition to reaching them, are most likely to generate some kind of participation before Jesus comes again in glory, even if someone starts out as a Spectator.

THOUGHT BYTES

To ensure that your strategy for using social media is as complete as possible, ask:

- Do we know how members of our church community already use social media?
- Are the ways members of our church community use social media in sync with the platforms we want to use?
- How do we more fully engage the more occasional users of social media?

Chapter 9 Curating and Creating Content

There's a reason why internet aficionados often invoke the aphorism "Content is king." Bill Gates asserted this back in 1996[19] and, although some technology observers have subsequently debated whether content still holds this majestic title, it doesn't really matter how you rank the importance of content—you'll need lots of it.

Not much of anything can happen online without some kind of content. Certainly nothing much can happen through social media without providing content that generates what digital strategists call engagement (i.e., interaction). There's a reason why it's called *social* media.

Content is the quasi-technical term for the stuff people will read, see, watch, listen to, or otherwise engage with because someone like you makes it available online.

There are essentially two ways to generate social media content. Either you develop and post original material or find existing goodies to share with others. People who develop original online content are known as "content creators." Those trolling the internet for interesting and useful tidbits are known as "content curators" and, no joke, this is a real job position that librarians are especially well qualified to fill. Some people do both. I do both and have earned my so-called living at times by doing both.

You want and will need both types of content, although both can become suspect if it devolves into a never-ending stream of thinly veiled promotion. Resist that temptation! You'll get no-where very quickly if promoting the church website and getting more butts in the pews is your greatest goal. In the world of church, we need to create and curate content in the joyful hope of sharing the Gospel, ministering to others, and developing community.[20]

Likewise, all your efforts will come to naught if the content you post is of dubious value. Be prepared, as a matter of strategy, to define what constitutes success and then use tools provided by each social media platform to note what's working and what isn't. Ditch, delete, and discontinue posting what doesn't work.

And of course you want any and all your social media content, regardless of origin, to be quality content. But what, pray tell, does that mean?

Quality content easily and consistently generates interaction in the form of blog comments, "likes," re-tweets, and re-)ins. It's content your intended audience will save for further contem-plation and maybe even post to social bookmarking sites (e.g., Reddit, StumbleUpon, BuzzFeed, Delicious, Digg) for like-minded others to discover.

Quality content will enhance your audiences' knowledge, deepen their understanding, strengthen their faith, stimulate conversation, and build community. Change becomes possible when content helps visitors discover new aspects of self in re-lation to others. Community emerges when content stimulates interaction with and among online visitors.

In the world of church, quality social media content informs, educates, and inspires action that's Christ-centered and an-chored in Gospel values. With a reverential nod to St. Paul the Apostle, social media content does not boast, it is not proud, it is not rude, it is not self-seeking, and does not delight in evil, but rejoices in the truth (1 Cor 13:4-6).

THOUGHT BYTES

As you consider either creating or curating content for your social media platforms, ask:

- Will the content we create or curate enhance our ministerial efforts?
- Does the content we create or curate help build community?
- How can we ensure that our content is Christ-centered and anchored in Gospel values?

Chapter 10   Print Is Not Dead; It's Being Transfigured

When the conversation takes place by phone, I can easily imagine the other person's body language and facial expression. Clenched jaw. Pinched line between the eyebrows. A grimace that could double as a smirk. I know that arms would be crossed and hands would be fists if holding a phone wasn't involved. Maybe tears starting to well up. I've seen that happen when I've had this conversation in person.

Welcome to what I experience while discussing the dubious merits of relying on print publications to provide time-sensitive information these days. How often have I heard well-meaning church folk, including those working in communication ministry, announce that the printed newsletter or newspaper or magazine will be retired, "never" or "over my dead body." (Of course they mean their dead body, not mine. I think.)

If this exchange is face-to-face, I try to sound and look reassuring as I say, "No one is talking about totally eliminating print." I know fear when I see it and like to ease self-inflicted pain. "You'll still have print, but probably not in the same form."

It usually becomes a longer conversation. I'm fine with that. Whatever it takes to prove that I'm not the Grim Reaper of Print Publications, although I do feel put in that position at times.

Truth is I love print on many levels—creating it, editing it, reading it. Hey look! Here I am writing a book about digital media that will also be printed!

My print cred spans a few decades. It includes top-of-the-masthead editorial positions on newspapers and magazines starting when I was twelve (EIC of Tiger Tales!). My parents raised me to revere books. Writing, editing, and publishing them would come later. I was smitten with magazine writing until that market crashed. Blogging would become my salvation (see Chapter 14: Why Choose Blogging).

As for printing—actual printing—with type and ink and a press, I fell in love with that while a student at Rochester Institute of Technology at the School of Printing. In 2002, it was renamed the School of Print Media. In May 2012, it was renamed again, becoming the School of Media Sciences to embrace the reality of digital communications.

I mention this sequence of events to assert this: Print is not dead; it's being transfigured by digital technology. Transfigured . . . as in "changed in outward form or appearance." Transfigured . . . as synonymous with "renew" . . . as in You-Know-Who appearing. I prefer using the word "transfigured" because it also means "to change as to glorify or exalt."

In addition to being created in new ways (i.e., digitally), print is being *used* in new ways, especially relative to social media with which it has swapped positions in the pecking order.

Not so long ago, I'd print from screens so I could read and mark up hard copy. Now I'm so comfy with reading on a monitor that I have trouble seeing printed text. But next to my bed there is and will forever be a pile of books. I always turn to face the held-high Lectionary during the procession that opens worship. I consider untangling breviary ribbons part of praying the Liturgy of the Hours.

None of this changes my passion for online tools that make it possible to find and read online content. Conversely, my passion for tools for finding and reading pages upon pages of otherwise inaccessible and unavailable content online does not change my passion for print. There remains a place for both.

Times have changed and change continues as time goes on.

Once, print ruled. Social media, when it first arrived on the scene circa 2003, was the cupbearer. Now, when it comes to church communication, it's the other way around—or needs to be with print supporting social media efforts.

"Print oversized postcards with an invitation to join the conversation on your social media platforms," I counsel colleagues and clients. Why does any church's printed material land in anyone's snail mailbox without URLs (Uniform Resource Locator) for the church website and social media accounts? Add a QR (Quick Response) code and you make it easier for those with smartphones to visit your website or see anything else you want to promote.

Let's be clear: setting up an either/or scenario between print and digital media isn't necessary. You may and can, could and should, have both. Getting and staying ferociously positional obscures the greater goal, which is to communicate church and faith. It's a matter of knowing which works best for each audience.

Print is not dead; it's being transfigured.

 ## THOUGHT BYTES

Before continuing any major print publication like a newsletter, newspaper, or magazine, carefully consider whether doing so makes sense by asking:

- Does our audience really want and need this information in printed form?
- Is the design and content of our printed materials compelling enough to warrant the expense of production and mailing?
- How might clinging to print inhibit our outreach?

Chapter 11 Bridging the Digital Divide

Get involved with digital anything and at some point you'll find yourself discussing the gap between technology "haves" and "have-nots." This is what people generally mean when they talk about the "digital divide," an often invoked reason to shy away from social media. But there's more to the digital divide than lack of access due to poverty in the economic sense.

For a while, I experienced my own, very personal digital divide—with my father.

Always keen on technology, he was using a personal computer by the early 1980s. It was either an IBM PC or a Commodore. In either case, the thing was huge and weighed a ton. He used WordStar, a convoluted word processing program invented in 1978. I wanted nothing to do with any of it.

I was fine with advancing my then-career in academia by typing and retyping and retyping journal article manuscripts on my IBM Correcting Selectric II. A hulking clattering thing for sure, but still an exponential improvement over previous models requiring a substantial investment in correction fluid.

Computers? Too annoying. I'd had my fill of key-punching cards during graduate school so data could be run on mainframe computers that occupied entire floors, if not entire buildings.

Personal computers? Too expensive. I was already struggling on an assistant professor's salary. Also, too scary. I could not grasp the difference between hardware and software, terrified I'd blow up both, whatever the heck they were. And way too

Digital but Not Necessarily Social

The ever-expanding universe of digital tools includes ones that are not, technically speaking, forms of social media although they're transmitted and delivered via the internet. Your organization is probably already using one or more of the following:

- *E-newsletters:* regularly scheduled electronic communication providing news and information to an opt-in audience (e.g., for separate areas of ministry).
- *Email blasts:* electronic mailings sent simultaneously to a large, targeted group of people (e.g., for capital campaigns or special appeals).
- *Listservs:* mailing list software allowing subscribers to send email to one another on a special server through a designated account (e.g., to facilitate discussion among members of a ministry group).
- *SMS/Texting:* sending a concise message of up to 160 characters via mobile devices.

With the possible exception of listservs, which are becoming obsolete because they generate too much email, these are not considered social media because they do not generate real-time conversation. You cannot, for example, engage a community in conversation by responding to an email blast. Still, you must pay attention to how these digital tools fit into your communication strategy. In addition to their common use, make sure you launch none of these digital communication tools until you include:

- branded buttons for social media accounts;
- a compelling invitation to join ongoing conversations and groups on your social media accounts; and
- links that work!

The beauty of digital is that it allows everything to be seamlessly linked—but only if you link it and then promote those links. Remember, as people of faith, we do *not* have fans, friends, or followers. We *do* have potential partners in evangelism and ministry.

inconvenient. What was the point of learning a snazzy new tech solution to something that was already working laboriously well enough?

But my father would not shut up about the fabulousness of his computer. This was not only annoying but scary and inconvenient, especially because he was seventy years old and I was in my mid-thirties.

Eventually I broke down and bought my first computer, a Compaq portable that I dragged around on a luggage cart. I didn't use the computer for anything other than word processing. I had to draw the line somewhere and Google hadn't yet been invented anyway, so what else was there to do with a computer?

To summarize this saga: I didn't have money for a computer and didn't want to learn how to use one. Decades and many computers later, it's difficult for me to imagine being so scared and narrow-minded about technology, but I was.

Current debates about the digital divide revolve around these same two issues: (1) lack of access to computers as well as high-speed broadband and (2) lack of knowledge about computers and other digital technologies. Both situations are very real, although lack of access because of economic status seems to attract more attention.

True, the gap between technological haves and have-nots becomes a deep divide when high-speed broadband is unavailable or inaccessible because of cost. The cost of acquiring and maintaining up-to-date computer equipment also restricts internet access for the poor and homeless. It doesn't matter whether the church is located in an urban or a rural environment; lack of access is lack of access. Still, thanks to the prevalence of smartphones, the so-called digital divide is much smaller than the outcry would have you believe. Mobile is becoming the primary way people tap into online content, especially in developing countries.

Equally troubling for those of us in communication ministry is the gap between the "knows" and "don't-want-to-knows." Under the best of circumstances, fear masquerades as disinterest among many of those who would prefer to ignore social media. Under the worst, fear manifests as hostility. Meanwhile, technological triumphalism among the "knows" sometimes turns the gap into a chasm.

So how do we, as church, close the gap? How do we bridge the digital divide? The swift ascendancy of mobile technology—smartphones and applications developed for them—is making digital access relatively affordable and easy to use. While I'm loathe to cite research that will become obsolete before you finish reading this book, research reports from the Pew Internet Project reveal a future that's already here.

As noted in a 2012 report based on data collected at the close of 2011, the economically and educationally disadvantaged among us rely on their phones for just about everything.[21] The divide might not be closed but it is closing. We need to embrace what becomes possible as a result, like meeting and ministering to people where they are and with the technology they're most likely to use.

 THOUGHT BYTES

Instead of using the digital divide as an excuse to avoid using social media, commit to closing the gap by asking:

- What's the practical impact of the digital divide on our ability to generate community and enhance faith?
- What are we doing to increase access to digital technology for our congregants?
- How can we enhance computer literacy for our congregants?

Chapter 12   **Reaching Out to Special Populations**

Considering our commitment to welcoming the stranger and lifting up the downtrodden, our track record for making church accessible and community involvement possible for people with physical disabilities remains remarkably poor.

Church buildings, especially older ones, are simply not constructed to accommodate wheelchairs, scooters, and other assistive equipment. Materials such as printed worship booklets, announcement flyers, and bulletin boards cannot be read by those with severe visual impairments, let alone anyone who is blind.

Churches retrofitted with curb cuts, ramps, elevators, accessible toilets and grab bars in the bathrooms, braille signage, and the like might have these only because leadership understands the moral importance of making worship and community activities accessible. In the United States, churches are exempt under the Americans with Disabilities Act (ADA) from providing such accommodations.

This often comes as news to most people, including many ministers—ordained and lay. Do you see extra parking spaces, including those for wheelchair lift vans? Are service animals allowed to enter the building? Is American Sign Language provided during services? If so, these may have come to pass by the grace of Christian goodwill stimulated by fiercely illuminating encounters with disabilities rights activists.

Cultural barriers rooted in historic ignorance about the sources of physical, cognitive, and behavioral impairments have made the experience of church community equally inaccessible. Alas, there are still people of faith who confuse disability with illness. At best they chalk it up to God's will, at worst to demonic possession or spiritual warfare.

During the first decade of the twenty-first century especially, new technologies (e.g., voice recognition software) and the internet made it possible for people with visible as well as hidden disabilities to accomplish routine activities with less hassle. Now, social media offers unprecedented opportunities for active participation in community. And social media is democratizing. People with disabilities get to participate without disclosing their type of disability or if they have one at all.

Depending on the disability, some social media tools are better than others, but there are viable workarounds for ones you'd think wouldn't work at all, such as:

- providing closed captioning on and transcripts for YouTube videos to help people with hearing loss;
- including precise narrative descriptions on images to help the visually impaired;
- configuring hyperlinks embedded in blogs so that content pops up on the screen instead of opening in a new window requiring extra hand movements to navigate; and
- providing more descriptive text for hyperlinks (e.g., our schedule of activities v. click here).

And then there are social media platforms so good-to-go that lack of participation by people with disabilities has more to do with the church's culture of hospitality. Glory be, you can use social media to change that as well. Woe to the world because of stumbling blocks![22]

THOUGHT BYTES

Reaching out to as well as proactively accommodating people with disabilities is the ethically right thing to do. As you review online strategies and tools, ask:

- Do we generally understand and respond fully to the needs of people with disabilities?
- Are we willing and able to make special accommodations for people with disabilities without isolating them?
- How will the social media tools we choose welcome more participation by people with disabilities?

Chapter 13 Social Media Durability

Just when you think cyberspace could not possibly expand enough to hold another social media platform, a new one gets coded into being and launched into orbit. The universe of digital tools can seem mighty crowded, overwhelming at times. Which ones should you use to build church and faith? Why choose any of them? Which ones have staying power?

Start exploring the world of social media and you'll soon discover that most discussions focus on how to use these key platforms: Facebook, Twitter, Pinterest, and YouTube.

Savvy social media users will quickly point out that blogs should be on the list, as well as Instagram, Foursquare, and maybe Vimeo. Some will insist Google Plus must be included. Ever hear of Branch? It launched in public beta during August 2012 and of course I checked it out . . . for about thirty minutes. Who knows if and when it will become popular?

My personal list of essential platforms includes all of these minus Google Plus, which I pretty much ignore although I signed on when it was in private beta. I was wowed by its design until users started adding their voluminous, redundant content. My list includes LinkedIn, an important tool that's either underutilized or misused by clergy and churches. This is my list. For today. Next month, my list could be the same or completely different.

What hasn't and won't change are core features that will endure even when "must use" social media platforms change. What do they have in common?

By definition and therefore without exception, social media platforms make it possible to generate, build, and sustain conversations leading to relationships. Each and every one of them does this by allowing visitors to post original comments or reply to ones posted by someone else.

Even short, asynchronous comments can have impact. I've seen conversations gather momentum from something as simple as clicking the "like" button on a Facebook post or keying in "agree" after re-tweeting something on Twitter.

On Twitter you can see thought-provoking discussions develop after someone tweets "preach it!" You might be delighted (or appalled) to know I once generated a lively exchange among clergy from at least four denominations after adding "Jesus barfs" to something I'd re-tweeted about current events. I like to start and participate in frisky conversations; grim piety gives me heartburn and heartache.

Social media platforms are most durable when they can be used either separately or together as well as embedded into websites and e-newsletters. They're durable because there's

Choosing Social Media Tools					
	Blog	Facebook	Instagram/ Pinterest	Twitter	YouTube/ Vimeo
Announcements	✓	✓		✓	
Commemorating Events	✓	✓	✓		✓
Conversations		✓		✓	
Evergreen Information	✓		✓		✓
Planning Events	✓	✓		✓	
Reminders	✓	✓		✓	
Stories	✓		✓		✓
Time-Sensitive News		✓		✓	

remarkably little variation in how accounts get set up and the basic information users must provide.

As time goes by there seem to be fewer differences in navigation (e.g., how to find content and conversation) and functionality (e.g., how groups/lists are created, privacy settings). Design templates for user profiles and other features (e.g., tabs, drop-down menus) are becoming uniform across key platforms and more so as time speeds by.

As a practical matter, the proliferation of shared characteristics makes it relatively easy to shift from one platform to another. Learning one social media platform really well and keeping up with its modifications will significantly flatten the learning curve for almost any other tool you explore.

But please remember similarities in principle, function, and design do not render key platforms interchangeable. One will work better than another depending on your ministry, goals, and audience. Choosing social media requires knowing first and foremost whom you want to reach and what you hope to accomplish by doing so. Lord have mercy if you ignore this key step.

 ## THOUGHT BYTES

Social media options can seem overwhelming at first and enticing after you get comfy with using them. Before getting too enthralled with the next big social media thing, ask:

- How are we currently choosing which social media to use?
- What process will we use to decide whether to explore new social media platforms?
- Who will be responsible for deciding which and how many social media tools we'll use?

Chapter 14

Why Choose Blogging

Everything and everyone moves so quickly and time is at such a premium, especially online, that some social media fans can't remember when and why blogs emerged. We tend to forget that "web logs" developed during the mid-1990s and were mostly quirky online diaries written by individuals.

By the end of the 1990s, blogs had replaced bulletin boards and chat rooms as platforms for community building. Blogs provided a more spacious online environment to muse and amuse, which was then seen as a welcomed alternative to threaded conversations. Being able to post and respond to comments allowed communities to emerge between bloggers and readers, and often among readers as well.

Political, corporate, organizational, and group blogs didn't overpopulate the blogosphere until the early 2000s. Another half dozen years passed before blogs became recognized as a tool for mainstream reportage.[23]

I'm semi-embarrassed to admit that I didn't start blogging until 2007. It took me that long to get out of denial about the crashing print market. Within four years, I was managing two group blogs, had created two more personal ones, and was writing guest posts for many more. Blogging was a great outlet for working writers like me who weren't making money anyway for personal essays, book reviews, humor, and culture criticism. Not bitter. Love blogging.

By 2012, some tech culture critics were composing requiems for the blogosphere. You should feel free to ignore these declarations of demise, because when it comes to the world of church communication, blogging is still in its infancy. Yea verily, while you can find well-established blogs by clergy and theologians as well as religion book and magazine publishers, this is not the norm at local and diocesan/synodical levels. Church communicators are only now beginning to understand how blogs fit in the social media mix at the institutional level of church, assuming they have a social media mix.

To some extent this recent epiphany about the value of blogging for church is due to the cost of producing and mailing church print publications (see Chapter 10: Print Is Not Dead; It's Being Transfigured). Probably more significant is how blogs appeal to Baby Boomers and GenXers. Your congregants in these generational cohorts grew up reading articles in print. Now they want similar content delivered to their computers, tablets, and smartphones.

You already have blog content and know how to generate more. Adjusted for online readability, your blog content will come from feature stories, profile pieces, reviews, poetry, and prayers previously printed in your cost-prohibitive magazine or newspaper.

Whether a feature of the church website or set up as a standalone platform, church blogs work best when they provide: (1) content that attracts and interests new visitors and then inspires them to return; (2) a mechanism for conversation (i.e., comments); and (3) opportunities for visitors to connect via other social media tools (e.g., Facebook, Twitter, Pinterest).

Your church blog will not work well if it's used primarily for time-sensitive news and announcements; other digital platforms are much more effective for that content (see box: Digital but Not Necessarily Social, p. 49).

These additional factors make blogging a great choice for churches:

- Room for longer content makes blog writing especially appealing to the teachers, preachers, thinkers, prophets, and other storytellers in church communities.

- More than one blog can be created to focus on themes (e.g., more detailed commentary on Lectionary readings, liturgical seasons, sacramental prep) or audiences (e.g., youth ministry, adult faith formation, missions).
- Blogging platforms make it possible to post photos, videos, and podcasts as well as text.

Blogging in a church environment has its own special challenges, the most notable being ones involving editorial oversight and quality control.

Everyone needs an editor, but editorial oversight can get almighty touchy when you have a group blog with multiple contributors. Editing can become a proximate occasion of sin when contributors include clergy whose oral skills outshine their written ones. "We have several blogging bishops in my denomination," tweeted one priest during one of several church social media (#chsocm) chats on this topic. "Who is going to check their content? Who should?" Crickets.

Web-based communications are inherently visual, so explaining that text must be formatted for easy online reading can generate angst, especially for writers or editors who have only been published in print (see Chapter 24: A Bit of How-To about Writing Online Content).

Since engagement is generated with comments, you'll need to make some decisions about comment moderation and user verification. The most successful (i.e., powerful) blogs are ones where comments lead to active conversations. Should these conversations be monitored? Absolutely. Ever deleted? Maybe, but when? (See Appendix B: Yes, You Need a Social Media Policy.)

How will you word the invitation to comment? Some blogs clearly state that comments wandering off point may be deleted. I think comment codes on Christian blogs ought to invoke the Gospel in some way. For a blog I designed, visitors to the comment box were reminded: " 'This is my commandment, that you love one another as I have loved you.'—John 15:12. In other words, be nice!"[24]

Advocates of comment moderation and user verification point out how these gatekeeping mechanisms help keep conversations on course and eliminate spam. Opponents to comment moderation wait in joyful hope for the community to monitor and moderate itself. Alas, almost every blogger I know has ended up enabling comment moderation when Christian love becomes not so abiding online and, believe me, I've seen stunningly vicious exchanges on faith and religion blogs. Lord, have mercy. Christ, have mercy. Lord, have mercy.

All these practical details are well worth working out so that your words may go out and not return to you empty, but accomplish what you want it to do[25] . . . on your church's blog.

THOUGHT BYTES

Should every church establish a blog? Heavens, no. Before adding one or more blogs to your social media mix, ask:

- Which ministries, if any, would benefit from having a dedicated blog?
- Do we have the energy, time, and talent to maintain a consistent blogging presence for at least two years with fresh, new content?
- Will establishing and maintaining quality content become a source of strife?

Chapter 15 Why Choose Facebook

Who doesn't already know about Facebook? Back in 2010, its early history was chronicled in a big-budget, award-winning Hollywood movie called . . . wait for it . . . *The Social Network*. Simply put in a grandiose but accurate way, with one billion users as of October 2012, Facebook is the largest social networking platform in the known universe.

Analysts claim users spend approximately eight hours a month on Facebook visiting, friending, reading, listening to music, looking at pictures, watching videos, leaving comments, and playing games. Some people spend way more time on Facebook, others much less. Since launching in 2004, Facebook has managed to transform online communications as well as contemporary culture. Really, how else would "friending" and "liking" have become verbs?

I got started on Facebook when my high school graduating class (Go Tigers!) was planning a reunion. Someone set up a closed group that many visited on a regular basis for nearly a year in advance. By the time we got together IRL (in real life), we'd already gotten caught up on details and were therefore able to appreciate one another as the adults we'd become instead of the kids we'd once been.

During the past four years I've added people, organizations, and enhanced functionality to my account. And although Facebook has never become my go-to place for conversation and community, it reigns supreme on my list of must-have social media tools for ministry.

Facebook is great for church communication and ministry because in addition to providing an efficient, cost-effective way to broadcast news and publicize events, it provides many other options for generating and sustaining community (e.g., the time-line, groups, customizable tabs on the home page, notes, lists).

Posting announcements and prayer requests to the news feed, clicking "like," and adding comments are the most obvious ways to use Facebook.[26] But community is revealed, emerges, and can be enhanced when churches:

- provide an illustrated history of the community and its activities by populating the timeline with milestones and pictures;
- help congregants exchange ideas and chat in be-tween meetings by setting up open (public) groups for committees;
- create a safe haven for ministries requiring privacy and confidentiality by setting up closed (private) groups;
- reduce administrative hassles by using the Events func-tion to publicize celebrations and events, invite people, collect RSVPs, and send reminders;
- participate in the larger community of faith by "liking" pages of sister churches, denominational organiza-tions, and religion publishers and then leaving mean-ingful comments.

Community, which takes time to build online and off, will always emerge more readily if church leadership actively par-ticipates, especially from a place of relatable authenticity rather than one of distanced authority.

Clergy need to think through, in advance, whether it makes sense to set up two accounts. Some clerics who attend the weekly church social media (#chsocm) chat on Twitter make a strong case for putting forth an integrated identity with one Facebook account with carefully configured privacy settings. Others make an equally strong case for setting up a separate account for all church-related content and conversation. Different strategies, both with the goal of protecting self while honoring Self.

Most, if not all, of the concerns frequently raised by social media defeatists—privacy violations, data-mining, and being flooded with minutia—can be swiftly and easily handled by learning how to optimize Facebook settings. Experienced, knowledgeable users can help you with that as can subscribing to news from the supremely useful site Inside Facebook.[27]

What about Google+?

Lots of excitement in the world of social media when Google+ (aka, Google Plus) first rolled out in June 2011. Google+ allowed users to sort connections into discrete groups called circles, thereby controlling how to share information. The hangout feature allowed up to ten people to chat simultaneously via video. Other options included being able to send private messages and edit posts after publishing.

All features were touted as major improvements over Facebook. Within months, Facebook rolled out its timeline interface and made it easier to sort friends into lists. Privacy settings were refined and subscriptions introduced to further differentiate public and private sharing. Checkmate?

Meanwhile, Google+ was becoming deluged with comments longer than blog posts and duplicate content from other social media platforms. On the upside, hangouts became popular despite their size limit. Google+ recently introduced groups that users quickly set up and swarmed to for more focused conversation.

Should you bother with Google+? Some observers think it will eventually fizzle out like Google Buzz and Google Wave. Some think it will survive because it's a Google product. Time will tell and in the world of social media that means sooner rather than later.

Other concerns about how "Facebook is for kids" and "our older members won't use it" can be gently dismissed by explaining how that has radically changed. By the end of 2011, the most rapidly growing segment of Facebook users was comprised of people (mostly women) in their fifties and older. The exodus from Facebook of Millennials has given rise to the quip, "Facebook is the party your parents crashed."

Of all the expressed concerns, those about time management are probably the most legitimate. Facebook is constantly changing in response to users' requests and market demands, so it's not unusual to wake up one morning to find favorite features refined, replaced, or simply gone.[28] Most innovations really are announced in advance, which is why whoever is in charge of your church account needs to pay attention and follow at least one blog or tech news aggregator (e.g., MashableTech).

I realize this sounds like a lot of time-intensive work, but it's actually very manageable and need not take up more than a couple of hours each week. Of course it helps if the account administrator(s) love social media and consider church communication a ministry. Strange but true: I've encountered situations where the person responsible for church social media didn't like it and artfully avoided learning how to use it.

The effort it takes to set up, monitor, and maintain a Facebook account is well worth it; count on receiving rewards for what you have done. Turn away from all other social media if you must, but don't deny the value of Facebook.

THOUGHT BYTES

Moving forward with Facebook is, in almost every church situation, probably the best choice, but you'll still need to ask:

- How will we use Facebook to go beyond broadcasting news and events to build community among our various audiences?
- Which ministries would benefit from having groups and should those groups be open/public or closed/private?
- Who will have primary responsibility and authority for setting up and monitoring our Facebook page(s) and group(s)?

Chapter 16 Why Choose LinkedIn

Ah, LinkedIn, a social media platform for which I have special affection. While I'd participated within online communities as early as 1993, LinkedIn was where I fully succumbed to the nimble charms of twenty-first-century social media.

LinkedIn was established to serve social networking needs of professionals. Within a month of launching in 2003, LinkedIn had 4,500 members. By October 2012, it had become the world's largest online network for professionals with more than 187 million members.

I skipped other social networking sites and went directly to LinkedIn because of its focus on professional development. It made my résumé and references readily available. It provided ways for me to develop visibility, which I did by offering counsel about marketing communications, writing and editing, and ethics.

I built networks based on existing connections in various industries and started accumulating recommendations (references). Over the years, I've left some groups and joined others, added and deleted skill areas, and changed my position description. What hasn't changed is using it to stay focused on career and vocation-related information.

This strategy became even more important when cross-posting from Twitter or Facebook to LinkedIn became possible. No one on LinkedIn needs to know when I nap or that my cat is a full partner in my literary endeavors, and I actively discourage people from sharing their personal adventures. That's why Twitter and Facebook were created.

Church folk tend to either ignore LinkedIn, assuming it's only for business professionals and organizations, or create accounts with information so skimpy it's useless. So should you or your church/diocese/synod/faith-based organization bother with LinkedIn? Maybe.

Take a look at how other churches and mission-based non-profit organizations use it. Scroll through the hundreds of groups to find ones that might make sense to join. There are LinkedIn groups for church administrators, clergy by denomination and region, chaplains, clergy and lay leadership involved with technology, seminary alumnae, and more. There are secular groups that I urge anyone involved with church social media to join (e.g., Social Media Today).

If you join LinkedIn:

- craft a profile with more than basic information;
- be a professional among professionals;
- maintain stronger boundaries between work and personal life than you do on Twitter or Facebook; and
- join groups to which you can contribute and from which you can learn.

Also check out LinkedIn's "Company" page feature, an option that has been used by dioceses, synods, national churches, and faith-based organizations. This is an option for churches but involves thinking through additional issues like how to ensure whatever information you post about your church/organization is consistent across platforms (i.e., website, Facebook page).

THOUGHT BYTES

If you have very limited time and energy for social media, then LinkedIn should probably not be on your list of platforms to use. Still, before rejecting it entirely and forever, ask:

- What might I and/or my church community gain by having a presence on LinkedIn?
- If I and/or my church community join LinkedIn, how will we contribute and participate?
- Who will have the responsibility and authority for setting up and maintaining our institutional account?

Chapter 17 Why Choose Pinterest

At first Pinterest was viewed as yet another upstart social media tool with little appeal beyond its initial user base of artists, designers, photographers, crafters, and do-it-yourselfers.

Pinterest, after all, was just a virtual bulletin board onto which users could pin (i.e., post) images. How was *that* going to build community? Plus the majority of early adopters were women, which resulted in Pinterest being dismissed as too gender-specific. At first.

Much has changed, and changed dramatically, since Pinterest arrived on the social networking scene in 2010. Within two years of rollout, Pinterest had 11.7 million registered users. Millions more visit Pinterest without registering.

By the end of 2012, men had joined the ranks of pinners. It also became clear that, unlike other social media platforms, this one appealed to users across generational lines, with Millennials, GenXers, and Boomers pinning, re-pinning, liking, and commenting on the same visual content.

On Pinterest the focus is on images. In return, the images help visitors focus. What they focus on depends on the imagination, resourcefulness, and creativity of whoever manages a Pinterest account and sets up thematically organized boards. Community emerges as participants respond to one another's contributions. Here, the contribution is visual. Whatever text appears is mostly in the form of short, user-generated captions and comments rarely exceeding a few words. The option of setting up business accounts became available in 2013.

What about Instagram?

You'll often hear Instagram mentioned with reverence during discussions about social media. This might seem weird at first because Instagram is a smartphone picture posting application for iOS (Apple) and Android devices.

Instagram allows users to choose from more than a dozen fancy funky filters to enhance photos taken with smartphones. Those photos are then posted to other social networks (e.g., Facebook, Tumblr, Foursquare) in addition to Instagram.

So what makes it social? Once posted, the images prompt comments that, in some instances, can morph into fuller conversations, which in turn leads to community. Hashtags, the labeling convention developed on Twitter, are used to categorize content, making searching and finding easier for a special interest community.

If this doesn't convince you that Instagram is a social media tool, then perhaps this will: Facebook bought Instagram for approximately $1 billion (cash and stock) in March 2012. Instagram crossed the 100 million registered users mark by September 2012. The bad news? That purchase resulted in Instagram pulling its photos from Twitter and a kerfuffle about who owned the rights to images emerged in December 2012.

Who could have predicted Pinterest would so swiftly share first place with Facebook for the amount of time people spend on those sites each month?[29] How about anyone who understands the enduring appeal of images? This is certainly true for those attracted to churches anchored in a rich history of sacred art.

But online picture boards? Really? Absolutely.

Think about the bulletin boards in your church or religious education space. They may look cheesy, but don't people always seem to gravitate toward them? They attract visual learners (see Chapter 4: Learning Styles). These visual learners are also the congregants whose faith is deepened by encounters with Christian art and architecture.

You know these people! Their vacation photo albums are filled with images of churches, statues of saints, details of tapestries and vestments, crosses on steeples against cerulean skies. Favorite spiritual practices involve profound engagement with images, such as praying Stations of the Cross and gazing at icons. They join the Altar Guild to spend more time with sanctuary decor. And they're likely to participate in an online community via Pinterest, even if they reject all other social media tools as too complicated.

In my case, it was love at first pin. No surprise there since I'd spent much of childhood collecting stuff for my collage box and decorating school classrooms. Pinterest soon became my happy place to relax after a day of high-speed and high-volume interaction on other social media. I created boards for images of irises and owls, St. Mary Magdalene and St. Teresa of Avila, the archangel Gabriel. After Easter, I assembled "He is Risen . . . Now What?" During Pentecost, I created "Come, Holy Spirit, ASAP."

To test how Pinterest might be used to build community, I invited participants at the weekly Twitter-based church social media (#chsocm) chat to post images on group boards for "Stations of the Cross," "Church Windows," and "Jesus the Christ." Then I sat back, watching people who, because of denominational disputes, would probably never worship together or enthusiastically share their love of church and Christ through sacred art.

Pinterest is the obvious choice for those involved with worship and sacred arts, but don't limit its use to those ministries. In addition to being extremely simple to set up and use, Pinterest:

- supports preaching, teaching, and storytelling by using images to illustrate gospel messages of feeding the hungry, sheltering the homeless, and lifting up the brokenhearted;
- provides another way to introduce resources and ideas (e.g., pinning pictures of book covers, church supper-worthy food, crafts that could be used for faith formation activities) and staff (e.g., pinning staff pictures from the church website);

- allows congregants and clergy alike to learn about one another's interests, hopes, and dreams without words getting in the way or being misinterpreted;
- makes sacred art and expressions of faith accessible to an unchurched audience without using the freighted-with-meaning label "religion."

Like any other social media, Pinterest comes with its own set of cautions, most notably ones about intellectual property and copyright. Users soon raised concerns about how to deal with visual spam.

In response, Pinterest quickly revised its terms of service, acceptable use policy, and privacy policy, all of which are on the Pinterest site. I think these policies are well worth reading because they emphasize authenticity, respect for others, and user accountability in service to community, issues at the core of any conversation about using social media to build church and faith.

THOUGHT BYTES

Please do not hesitate to set up a Pinterest account for liturgical and sacred arts ministries. You should probably also get one going for faith formation ASAP. And while you're doing that, ask:

- How could we use images to evangelize and reach out to others?
- Which other ministries would most benefit from sharing its mission via images?
- Who could we invite to group boards to promote ecumenism and interfaith communication?

Chapter 18 Why Choose Twitter

By the time this goes to press, Twitter's nimble far-flung power to provide real-time communications during political upheavals, weather emergencies, health crises, national trage-dies, and other worldwide events should be established enough to stop smart people from railing against it. That's my hope, one being fulfilled in the secular world. These days even mainstream broadcast networks feature on-screen hashtags so viewers may participate in Twitter-based conversations. Twitter has become mainstream. For church? Not so much.

Twitter is a real-time social media tool for finding and sharing interesting content as well as participating in conversations (see Chapter 8: Participants and Participation). It was originally char-acterized as "micro-blogging" because tweets (i.e., messages) are limited to 140 characters. And trust me when I tell you that a lot can be packed into 140 characters!

In the beginning, users were prompted with, "What are you doing?" Now a box simply appears with the phrase "Compose new Tweet," yet another indicator of how routine Twitter use has become. Still, if you're completely new to Twitter, it's a learning-by-doing medium that's likely to drive you batty until you've tried it for a while.

It can take a few weeks of steady use before the power and glory of Twitter is fully revealed. At first glance, Twitter seems to be an endless stream of blather, random comments, and links to content without context. With regular use, disconnected con-versations suddenly become coherent. Twitter works well for visual-kinesthetic learners for whom typing short-form content is an easy-breezy way of communicating. Twitter is a Godsend for self-avowed introverts (see Chapter 5: Personality Types).

I'd been using Twitter for a month before having my own "aha" moment. The angels came down and the choir sang for me during the 2008 presidential debates—relative to Twitter, not US politics.

As I watched a fast-moving stream of tweets, laughing at some and groaning at others, I realized I had stumbled into the largest living room on the planet, one filled with often brilliant, sometimes absurd but always engaging, commentary and conversation. Not for nothing has Twitter been characterized as an online dinner party with an amazing assortment of guests.

Me? I absolutely love Twitter. If and when it disappears, I'll be sad and then immediately embrace whatever social media platform provides real-time, short-form communication.

At the same time, I readily admit that Twitter may not be the optimal choice for local churches. It works best when used for a combination of content, commentary, and conversation. Dioceses, synods, and national church organizations can productively use it as a link-to-content news feed, but only if at least one person on staff is willing to set up, find material for, and monitor the account. You need to know that even if there's abundant willingness, a well-managed Twitter account will take up someone's time, energy, creativity, and focus at any level of church.

Thou Shalt Not . . .

For the love of all that is holy, do *not* post anything that:

- you want to keep private;
- puts you at risk for hostile ridicule;
- forces you to take action you cannot take;
- jeopardizes your ministry; or
- will make Jesus weep.

Still, there are very good reasons to choose Twitter. It's an effective and productive choice when individuals set up personal accounts and commit to acting as ambassadors for church and faith by:

- tweeting about church events, programs, and activities that might attract visitors;
- participating in regular and formal Twitter-based conversations (i.e., tweetchats) devoted to Bible study, ministerial efforts, theological inquiries, and denominational concerns (see Chapter 22: A Bit of How-To about Tweetchats);
- attending and contributing to church-related conferences, conventions, assemblies, and other convocations by using relevant hashtags;
- tweeting or re-tweeting prayers as well as words of wisdom from sermons; and
- contributing links to web-based content and images that enhance spiritual and faith formation.

Even more powerful than using these time-tested ways is how Twitter allows people of faith to connect with one another across denominations. This comment by a participant in the weekly Twitter-based chat about church social media (#chsocm) is typical: "Twitter has broadened my ecumenical world and deepened my faith with the richness of others' experiences." Personally, I've witnessed and been privileged to participate in conversations whose authenticity, poignancy, intelligence, faithfulness, and laugh-out-loud humor are as equal to any I've encountered in so-called "real life."

On Twitter, conversations generate relationships; groups form and communities emerge (see Chapter 6: Virtual Community Is Real Community). Church is no longer confined to or contingent upon a building. For followers of Jesus the Christ, Twitter breathes new life into the words "follow me."

THOUGHT BYTES

Still think you need to set up an institutional account for your church on Twitter? If so, ask:

- How could we, as an organization, best contribute to Twitter relative to content and conversation?
- Which of our ministries or events would be enhanced by being tagged, then promoted and discussed on Twitter?
- Who will be responsible for finding, creating, and posting content; engaging in conversations with other individuals or groups; and monitoring our Twitter account?

Chapter 19   Why Choose YouTube

Our ancestors were transfixed by the sight of shadows moving across cave walls; later generations have been held in slack-jaw captivation by movies and then television. We love moving pictures, especially when audio is added. YouTube's popularity should come as no big surprise.

According to claims that YouTube made on its statistics page, every week many millions of people take some kind of social action as a result of watching a video. That's a lot of likes, shares, and comments on the YouTube site itself. Now add to that the interaction generated by videos subsequently posted to blogs, Facebook, Twitter, and Pinterest.

Clearly YouTube is an important platform, one you'll want to add to your church social media mix for two major reasons. First, videos are an effective way to reach audio-visual learners, those who best retain information by hearing and seeing, listening and watching. Second, unlike other social networking platforms that appeal to specific cohorts, videos are watched, bookmarked, and shared by viewers across generations. And don't forget, YouTube is perfect for finding instructional videos about setting up and using social media.

As is the case with all social media, whether and how you use video depends on what you want to accomplish. Figure that out and one of two options emerges. You can either produce your own videos or may use videos produced by others.

Video production is not an expensive enterprise. These days perfectly fine video can be shot from a smartphone, free or inexpensive editing software is available online, and distribution is free. Your more significant investment will be time.

The challenge for church at all levels is producing useful, engaging videos. In practical terms this means creating content short enough to watch in no more than five minutes, preferably less than three when shooting interviews or commentary. This is what takes time. Lots of time.

Case in point: I easily spent twelve to fifteen hours creating "Social Media: Don't Be That Church," which was 1:28 (i.e., one minute and twenty-eight seconds long).[30] Granted, some of that time was spent getting up to speed with the XtraNormal, a free text-to-movie platform. My second XtraNormal video, running 1:20, "Don't Be That Church II: We Need a New Website," took about six delightful hours to create.[31]

Fortunately, YouTube videos don't have to be super slick. In fact, anecdotal evidence suggests viewers respond more

What about Vimeo?

At some point in the process of setting up and populating a YouTube account, someone who knows about such things might ask, "What about Vimeo?"

Often characterized as "hipster YouTube," Vimeo is known for posting high quality, high definition (HD) digital videos on its site. It has always focused on quality content from users. Independent videographers welcomed its ban on advertising.

Generally speaking, Vimeo is favored by those keen on aesthetics and more committed to embedding videos on their sites than reaching a far-flung audience of potential viewers.

Vimeo has been on the scene since 2004 and by January 2012 claimed to have 9.7 million registered users and 65 million unique visitors a month. YouTube, owned by Google, gets approximately 1 billion unique visitors a month.

Which is the right choice for your church? My standard answer applies: it depends on your goal(s) and audience(s)—your strategy!

favorably to videos produced by competent amateurs than they do to ones produced by professionals.

Your church's videos need to be easy to see and hear. And have I mentioned they must be short? They must be short. Brief. Edited way down. This can be painful for those who think every

---

Choosing Social Media for Personal Use?
Know Thyself!

The social media tools you choose to build church community may not be the best ones for personal use. The more you know about yourself, the better equipped you'll be for choosing among available options.

If you're new to social media or feeling stuck with choices you've already made, I recommend creating a mini-retreat for yourself. Light candles, play some Benedictine chant in the background, pray for wisdom as you explore these core issues:

- How do you best receive and retain information? Are you a visual, auditory, or kinesthetic learner?
- What's your favorite mode of communication? Would you rather talk on the phone, write a lengthy email, or send a text message?
- Are you energized by interacting with lots of people or do you prefer observing and listening? Do you prefer community or solitude?
- How do you typically find God in your life? Are you engaged primarily at a sensory level or a cognitive one? If both, then in what proportion?

These are questions I ask whenever people tell me they've tried social media and it "didn't work" or they "hated" it. Without fail, I discover they've chosen a social media tool that's fundamentally incompatible with how they typically engage with the world and seek God.

Know thyself . . . and then choose social media platforms for personal use from that vantage point.

precious moment of the Christmas pageant is, uh, precious. Videos also need to be titled, described, and tagged so anyone can find them.

But you don't have to produce original videos to benefit from YouTube. Use the site to find content to then post on your website, blog(s), Facebook page(s), and maybe even to Pinterest. Think about searching for videos about:

- Christianity, church history, and Scripture study to support religious education;
- baptism, Eucharist, and confirmation to support sacramental preparation; and
- mission activities and ways to serve within and beyond the local church to build community.

And look for videos of:

- worship experiences, sacramental celebrations, and people talking about God's presence in their lives to enhance faith formation; and
- traditional and contemporary hymns, anthems, and chant to generate joy and gratitude.

God knows there's no shortage of things to hear and watch in the world of church. Sermons and celebrations come immediately to mind although these may not, in fact, be the best way to spend your YouTube capital. "Remember that YouTube isn't a second pulpit for the pastor," cautioned one participant during a church social media (#chsocm) chat on the topic of using videos to communicate church and faith.[32] "Thou shall not be boring," proclaimed another. And to that, the people tweeted, "Amen."

THOUGHT BYTES

Without a doubt, video content is a powerful, cost-effective way to educate and inspire. YouTube is a well-established social media platform, but to help you decide how best to use it, ask:

- How will we use video to build church community?
- Are we willing and able to create original video content?
- Which ministries would benefit from using video content that already exists?

SECTION III

MAKING SOCIAL MEDIA WORK

Chapter 20   Integrating Social Media

Take another lovingly critical look at your website, social media accounts, e-newsletters, and e-pistles from your pastor or bishop. Would anyone know these communication materials are from the same church?

Not just social media but everything you create to communicate church and faith must look and sound like it's being launched from the same organization, or at least from the same faith. Marketers call this "branding," a term that worries some church people who cry out to the echo chamber, "Jesus isn't a brand!" and "Church isn't a business!" and "Market segmentation undermines Christian unity!"[33]

Let me provide solace and comfort by explaining that those of us involved with marketing communications for churches are absolutely not interested in commodifying or commercializing Our Lord and Savior, Jesus the Christ. What we call a "brand" could as easily and more palatably be called an "identity."

In either case, we're committed to ensuring that who we are and what we believe is conveyed clearly, consistently, and coherently. Words and deeds plus the tools we use to announce and promote must be in alignment. And given what we know about how people access information, materials need to work equally well for visual, auditory, and kinesthetic learners (see Chapter 4: Learning Styles).

Remember, social media is not something separate, a nice-to-have add-on to your church website. It's an essential tool for communicating faith and building community in between worship services and committee meetings. Social media gives potential newcomers ways to observe how your community interacts. To that great and glorious end you want to integrate every social media tool you use across platforms and with other

---

The We'll-Get-to-It-Someday Website

Praise be to Google from which all online destinations flow, visitors have found your website.

Now what?

Can they find anything on it? Information up-to-date? Content readable without endless scrolling down the screen? Design clean and classically contemporary without being too trendy? Are visitors able to register online for programs and events? Do they know where, how, and *why* to join your community conversation on social media?

"No" to all the above? You're in remarkably good company. That background sound? Jesus weeping.

Far too many churches, dioceses, synods, and faith-based organizations slog along with something that, most kindly put, is below substandard. Behold what I call the "we'll-get-to-it-someday" website. Excuses abound for this sorry state of online conditions: no money, no skills, and, my personal favorite, no one knows how to code HTML.

I bring glad tidings! These days you do not need buckets of money to redesign, rewrite content for, and load a highly functional, easy-to-navigate website onto a content management system (CMS) platform that doesn't require HTML skills. Really, I'm not making this up.

Get on with the ministry of building church and faith using social media, but do not put off fixing your website. First, get it assessed for navigation (i.e., how to find stuff), functionality (i.e., how to do stuff), design, and readability. Then, get it updated ASAP.

Your website is the first place online seekers will visit, so make sure they'll stay to learn more and then leave knowing who you are, what you offer, and how to get more involved in person as well as through social media.

vehicles for communication, digital and print. Think seamless garment. One that looks good.

Establishing a style guide for editorial guidelines and a brand book for design will help you do this (see Chapter 27: Best Practices for Digital Ministry). And while you're at it, you must know enough about digital platforms, how they work and your audience, to distribute content onto the ones best suited for showcasing that content. You'll make it easier for congregants and visitors to understand who you are and what you're doing by posting:

- basic information and concisely written educational content on the website;
- time-sensitive news and information in e-newsletters;
- inspirational, thought-provoking, and community-building content and conversation on blogs and Facebook (in either private or open groups); and
- audio-visual content on YouTube and cross-posted to blogs, Facebook, and possibly Twitter.

Of course individual ministries within a church may develop their own "look" because each ministry has its own audience and goals, even if the message about living a life of faith is the same. But be careful about creating too many special distinct identities. Disconnects emerge when ministries set up blogs and Facebook pages so unique that no one would know they're from the same church community.

Sometimes this has more to do with how people seem to gravitate toward ownership, thinking "my ministry" while saying "our church." If this is going on, then proceed with pastoral care. You've moved away from a conversation about why and how to use social media. Perhaps it's time for a prayerful conversation about becoming and behaving like One Body in Christ.

THOUGHT BYTES

Even if you've already committed to creating a style guide and brand book, or using one already created by another church, take a look at your social media accounts and ask:

- How would visitors to our social media accounts know they're visiting ministries within the same organization?
- What have we done to ensure that our logo, avatar, descriptive text, contact information, disclaimers, banner images, and color palette are consistent across social media platforms?
- What needs to happen for us to get all our digital tools in alignment?

Chapter 21   Managing Social Media on Multiple Platforms

Now that you've set up social media accounts, how will you keep them filled with content, monitor conversations, and coordinate everything? Do not be afraid. Although it may seem overwhelming, sustaining a well-coordinated public presence with multiple accounts within and across multiple platforms is not a big deal. Trust me, keeping track of breviary ribbons is more complicated.

In fact, it's pretty easy to manage social media on multiple platforms because online services have been developed for this very purpose. Alleluia, amen! These digital tools make it possible for one person to do the work of many without having to worry too much about pesky details like dates, time zones, or being anywhere near a desktop computer.

The top-rated online services for managing social media will change over time. Such is the nature of digital technology. But for as long as they're around, I recommend using any of the following to distribute and manage social media content. All work equally well for personal and institutional accounts. All supply free versions with easy-to-follow tutorials. Some offer paid upgrades with extra features that you probably won't need for a local church but would be helpful at the regional or national level. And when the ones I've listed below disappear, I'm confident you'll have no problem finding others just like them:

- *Buffer:* schedules and automatically posts content to multiple social media platforms.
- *Tweetdeck, HootSuite, and Twubs:* services that help users find, follow, and contribute to hashtagged conversations/chats on Twitter.

Making Social Media Manageable for Personal Use

Worried about getting trapped in an inescapable social media vortex? This won't happen if you remember that whatever systems you've created for offline communication can be easily adapted for online use.

Think about how you routinely engage with the world. How often, at what time of day or night, and for how long do you typically chat by phone, participate in group activities, read newspapers or watch TV to follow current events, flip through magazines to find household hints and decorating tips or recipes, pray with Scripture or other inspirational writings?

Now, take what you already know about the rhythm and flow of your offline life and use it to make social media manageable for personal use.

For example, if you read newspapers in the morning and watch news broadcasts at 11:00 p.m., then stick to that schedule if you use Twitter as a news feed. If you listen to CNN or news radio all the time, then go ahead and scan Twitter without ceasing. If you set aside time every few days to read magazines, then make that your schedule for reading blogs, e-zines, and e-newsletters. Do your phone conversations with friends and family tend to go on and on? If so, then don't worry about spending the same amount of time chatting with friends and family on Facebook or Twitter.

Do not demonize social media. It's not an evil time suck but simply another way to communicate. Social media savvy friends can help you get comfy with these tools, providing useful tips for integrating these tools into daily life. If, after giving different types of social media a fair trial, you don't like any of them, then opt out for personal use and do not volunteer to manage social media for your church.

- *Tweetdeck, HootSuite, Seesmic:* all services manage content from, post content to, and monitor content on multiple accounts within social media platforms as well as across multiple platforms.

Remember too that all social media platforms include features for organizing and managing the flow of content within them as well as ways of linking content among them. For example, you can set up your blog feed so links to new posts automagically appear on Facebook and Twitter, configure Twitter to post tweets on Facebook, adjust Pinterest settings so images you've pinned show up on your Facebook timeline, and so forth and so on and on in a virtual round-robin of cross-platform posting.[34]

These services are great social media management tools.

Find them, install them, and learn how to use them. They'll make it easier to juggle social media accounts and deliver content swiftly. As a result, you'll end up having more time to keep content fresh and conversations going in the sure and certain hope that community will emerge.

 THOUGHT BYTES

Before setting up social media accounts, ask:

- Do we want or need to have multiple accounts within and across platforms?
- Have we carefully thought through the tactical issues of setting up multiple accounts within and across platforms (see Appendix A: Strategic Choices)?
- What will we do to ensure the smooth management of our accounts?

Chapter 22   **A Bit of How-To about Tweetchats**

Although I do tend toward extraordinary hyperbole, I'm not exaggerating when I say that at this point in my life nearly all my most treasured friends and colleagues are ones I've met on Twitter. Many started out as interesting people with whom I'd swap resources. They became colleagues as we discovered and discussed mutual interests, especially in the realm of vocation. Now they're dear friends with whom I share wows and woes. They're my go-to people for counsel that I request publicly so others benefit from shared wisdom. They're my trusted community for reality checks and prayer support that I tend to request through "back channel" to protect my privacy.

After four-plus years on Twitter, I've met quite a few online contacts face-to-face. Whenever I do, I marvel at our strong connection and how conversation becomes seamlessly possible during these tweetups (i.e., gathering of people who have met via Twitter). If we share a meal, I'll already know if bacon, chocolate, and coffee will be involved. Real presence attains new meaning in these moments.

Meanwhile, there are dozens of people I haven't met and will probably never meet, but we share an equally strong bond thanks, in great part, to weekly tweetchats (see Chapter 6: Virtual Community Is Real Community). These are Twitter-based conversations among tweeple with shared interests and concerns using a hashtag (#) for easy identification (e.g., #chsocm for church

> **Top Technical Barriers to Social Media Success**
>
> While it's true that smaller churches often struggle to pur-
> chase and maintain equipment and services, it's also true that
> larger ones with considerable resources sustain technical
> barriers. Social media success is undermined when:
>
> - the website is outdated in terms of platform, functional-
>   ity, design, and content;
> - WiFi has not been enabled throughout the church, or
>   access to it is limited to a few leaders; or
> - training staff and congregants to find and use online
>   resources is considered a nonessential luxury.

social media, #blogchat for blogging, #ToolsChat for online tools
and technologies, #mobilechat for mobile strategies and tactics).

Although individuals and organizations will organize tempo-
rary topic-specific tweetchats, most meet weekly and have for
a couple of years. These moderated conversations typically last
for an hour on the clock, much longer if you track what happens after and in between tweetchats.[35] Because these chats
show up in the public Twitter stream they are by default, if not
intent, open to anyone, which means church-based chats are
not restricted to ordained clergy and vowed religious. "Nones"
may and do participate!

In addition to being an effective way to meet people, tweetchats provide a great way to see, in action, the power of a
threaded conversation, even ones limited to 140 characters per
exchange. Follow enough of these and you'll be amazed at how
focused an exchange can get when all the throat-clearing and
other blah-blah that goes on during in-person conversations
and meetings has to be jettisoned.

People who have difficulty grasping the point of Twitter tend
to develop more appreciation for its community-building value
after attending a few consecutive tweetchats.

At first, the pace of these somewhat unthreaded conversations can be daunting to newcomers, which is why observing is easier than fully participating at the beginning. Fortunately, there are ways to manage the fast flow of information and conversation (see Chapter 21: Managing Social Media on Multiple Platforms), so don't worry about that. Arrive when you can, leave when you must, jump into the conversation at any time.

In general, Twitter-based chats are rollicking good fun, although every once in a while a topic will reveal areas of tension or disagreement among participants. Under the best of circumstances, the community defaults to universally recognized rules of engagement that include norms about civility and staying on topic. Under the worst, the moderator will publicly or privately tell the troublemaker to knock it off. Long-standing chats have survived over time because they're friendly communities that welcome newcomers and tolerate reasonable, thought-provoking disruption.

Tweetchats have emerged for any imaginable topic within and outside the world of social media, church, or social media and the church. Check out #knitchat, if you like to knit! You can find denominationally specific chats (e.g., #dreamumc [United Methodist Church] and #dreamPCUSA [Presbyterian Church USA]). Ecumenical, topic-based tweetchats emerge on a regular basis (e.g., #socmedchap, a chat for chaplains). For a while, a group of Presbyterian clergy set up #pttalk as a virtual presbytery and gathered for mutual support. While writing this, a tweet popped up on my Tweetdeck from an Episcopalian in lay ecclesial ministry. Was anyone interested in having a tweetchat about hands-on arts and crafts activities for Sunday school?

Search through one of the hashtag directories you can find with Google to discover tweetchats in topic areas. Put a query into the public Twitter stream for recommendations and watch suggestions pop up. Or, you can always start one. I did! There are plenty of social media evangelists who will be happy to help you get involved with this form of digital ministry.

THOUGHT BYTES

You're already participating in a number of activities, conversations, and communities. To decide whether to add tweetchats to your list, ask:

- What could I learn from others by participating in a tweetchat?
- Given my personality and learning style, would it make more sense to observe or participate in tweetchats?
- How might setting up a Twitter-based chat help us generate or continue important conversations?

Chapter 23 Jargon Alert

Social media will not work if what you communicate cannot be easily understood by regular folk, including those who do not necessarily consider themselves religious. Watch out for when and how you use jargon. You're probably using plenty. You're in good company because every group compresses worlds of meaning into terms that are immediately recognizable as being from or about that group.

So what's the big problem?

The big problem is jargon soon takes on a life of its own, tending to increase in amount and density as groups turn into communities. By the time a community becomes formalized as an organization (e.g., church) or social institution (e.g., religion) an entire esoteric vocabulary and way of speaking has become established.

To be fair, jargon serves a number of laudable functions for groups and its members by:

- allowing conversations to flow more efficiently;
- generating feelings of belonging;
- giving those who wish to belong yet another special thing to embrace; and
- generating and sustaining identity.

But while delivering these benefits to members jargon confuses and excludes everyone else. Not exactly optimal for ministry either off or online.

Please note that I'm not referring to using denominationally specific, commonly used terms that enhance comprehension, although these will need to be translated if you're committed to working ecumenically.[36] Nor am I recommending that our vocabulary of faith at its most lyrical be completely abandoned. We not-so-simply need to become more clear about when our most-loved language has become incomprehensible to those we hope to reach and inspire.

Jargon is especially deadly when it appears via social media, which requires short, clear, engaging communications. To make social media work you must get rid of jargon.

Yes, this is easier proclaimed than accomplished because churchy-church language so pervades the way people of faith speak and write that many are rendered inarticulate without it.

You can check this out by (nicely) asking, "What does that mean?" the next time you hear anyone using these fine examples of church speak: witness, called, evangelization, covenant, formation, mystery.

Business jargon has also wormed its way into communication among and emanating from church leadership. Try getting folks to define what they mean by transparency, accountability, innovation, authenticity. But don't stop there; push a bit further by asking, "How would we know that we've accomplished [jargon]?"

The good news is that stripping jargon from digital (and print) communication is easier than expunging it from daily conversation once you:

- create a style guide that identifies jargon that should not be used and provides more easily understood word/phrase substitutes;
- follow best practices for online writing (see Chapter 24: A Bit of How-To about Writing Online Content); and
- find and use an online tool to test readability.

And if reading this brief screed about renouncing jargon is putting a burden on your heart, then offer that up or put it at the foot of the cross—without uttering those cherished idioms, of course!

THOUGHT BYTES

If you love the language of church and are reluctant to remove most of it from your digital (and print, please) communication, make time to ask:

- Given our goals for using social media, how is using church speak useful or a deterrent?
- Who could help us become more aware of and evaluate our communication for churchy-church jargon?
- What might be in the way of our willingness or ability to refrain from using jargon?

Chapter 24 A Bit of How-To about Writing Online Content

Writing for the internet is quite unlike writing for print, something I needed to learn before I could land paying gigs writing web content. Since it would be read on a screen, text had to be written and formatted to optimize online readability. It had to be brief so readers wouldn't need to scroll down the screen. Sentences could be incomplete. And, only a few words.

Paragraphs could be one sentence or one word.

Seriously.

This is what writing for online readability looks like.

As for style, anything informative, educational, or inspirational needed to be warm, inviting, and lively. I quickly got into the habit of converting everything from passive to active voice, stripping the words "that," "to be," and "in order to" from almost everything I wrote.

Because I'd already logged time writing short, snappy magazine and ad copy, my transition from print to web was relatively painless. Not so for those whose primary communication is oral (e.g., clergy) or whose style of writing is complex (e.g., theologians and academicians). Neither length nor heft is a problem when writing for e-zines or publications that simply make their print issues available online. Both become big problems when writing blog posts or e-newsletter items.

Blog posts need to be short (i.e., 300 to 500 words). E-newsletter items must be even shorter (25–150 words), although you can get away with a bit more in both formats if some content is listed in bullet points.

When I'm the editor, I ask (read: tell) writers to break lengthy blog posts into a series of shorter ones that can be run over a number of days or weeks. I've been known to toss a prayer in the direction of St. Jude if I'm working with anyone who seems way too invested in preserving all text as originally written, so help them God.

Now that mobile has arrived on the scene, yet another set of rules have emerged for writing online content.

Measuring Social Media Success

How do you measure social media success? Tracking conversations, comments, likes, re-tweets, and re-pins will give you some sense of audience engagement. Almost every social media platform provides analytics, the fancy-pants term for discovering and communicating meaningful patterns in data.

Facebook, for example, makes extensive, high-level data about audiences readily available to page administrators. Blogging platforms provide detailed information about the numbers and sources of visitors. Any online service you use for managing social media will provide data about the size and online behavior of your target audiences, in addition to revealing reach (i.e., number of different people in your audience) and frequency (i.e., number of times your audience is exposed to your message).

Now what will you do with this information?

There are many ways to craft truth and meaning with numbers if that's your goal. The data you collect can be downloaded into businesslike spreadsheets or graphs. Go ahead and do that if you must, but this central question still remains: Why do you want to? If it's only to have so-called hard data to justify your social media existence, then you probably have a bigger problem to tackle—like discovering when, why, and how numbers became more important than mission and ministry.

Mobile devices have significantly smaller screens and content is navigated by touch. This means visitors who can view less content to begin with will see even less than that when their fingers block out part of the screen. And that screen keeps moving—scrolling up and down, being pulled in and out horizontally. This, in turn, raises design issues but here I'm zooming in on writing.

Brace and possibly cross (+) yourself. Whatever distress you may feel about low word count requirements for effective blogging and Facebook posts is about to intensify.

To maximize reading comprehension on a mobile device: (1) sentences need to be short, no more than fourteen words long; (2) words need to be three or fewer syllables; and (3) paragraphs may be two sentences long but making them one short sentence is more effective.

These specs are not a problem for experienced digital content writers and will be viewed as a delightful challenge by anyone who remains unfazed by the 140-character limits of Twitter. Everyone else needs to muster the willingness either to get trained or be edited.

 ## THOUGHT BYTES

You've always been known as a good writer and received positive feedback about your pieces in print publications. Before starting or plowing ahead with your blog, e-newsletter, or anything else for online consumption, ask:

- Given the realities of how people consume online content, how does my writing need to change for the web?
- What might be getting in the way of my taking a workshop or webinar focused on web-based writing?
- Who among my colleagues and friends could help me make my web-based writing more readable?

Chapter 25 Managing Online Conflict

Online conflict becomes much easier to manage once you understand that community dynamics remain constant regardless of location. Online, offline? Makes no difference—really and virtually. Humans are involved. Conflict is inevitable. Spend any time online and you'll soon encounter conflict in the form of bickering, disagreements, disputes, and full-blown battles with horrid spelling and egregious errors in grammar.

You can see when and how things get heated by reading through comments posted to blogs and YouTube, or by following the stream on Twitter for any hot topic that has been hashtagged (e.g., #GunControl). On Facebook, you're likely to find mild grousing on individual pages. For fierce fights, scan through public group pages, especially those set up to promote causes. Conflict emerges on those because they're *group* pages.

Social media works whenever you use the comforting knowledge that virtual community is real community to guide your response to and management of conflict when it emerges online (see Chapter 6: Virtual Community Is Real Community). You already know that people pick fights when they're feeling dissed—disregarded, dismissed, disrespected—or fearful that this might be going on. Tap into what you already know about responding to someone whose pain manifests as anger? Digital ministry!

You also need to think through what usually guides your reconciliation efforts. How do you typically behave in the world of church and beyond? If you're new to a community, how long do you wait before calling out what you perceive as bad behavior?

"Nothing Is Concealed That Will Not Be Revealed . . ."

Privacy is a much-cherished human right so fundamental that it's written into the United States Constitution. We expect our personal lives to be ours, free from intrusion and protected from public view and scrutiny. We expect to control what others know about us by deciding what to share as well as when, how, and with whom to share it.

At this point in history, these expectations are unrealistic.

Privacy has become completely transformed, which is to say it's a concept nearly devoid of meaning.

Blame the internet if you like, but that won't change today's cultural reality. Many GenXers and Millennials (aka, Digital Natives) ignore long-recognized boundaries between public and private, often dismissing them as absurd and obstructionistic. These cohorts are open about things that make older generations cringe. And I'm not just talking about partying and hooking up. They freely and vividly share disappointments, frustrations, and anger with individuals as well as social institutions. They do this in person and most certainly via social media. What's public? Everything. What should be private? Basically nothing.

This frequently shocks leaders who have traditionally had the authority to monitor and often control the flow of information. Historically, church leadership has been privileged with this authority, but if you have it, please do not use it to shut down internet access or banish social media.

Better choices: (1) acknowledge this significant cultural shift in how privacy is understood; and (2) accommodate our new reality by creating practical, actionable guidelines for internet use. Trying to shut down conversations by fiat or force will only generate the fear that leads to secrecy and other forms of soul- and institution-damaging dishonesty.

If other group members are handling the situation, do you jump in or let it be? How would you lead a group process to deal with someone causing trouble for themselves and others?

So far I've focused on group conflict but how about when conflict is—or seems—personal? Are you conflict-averse, hoping it's not happening and that it will fade away without your active intervention? Once you decide to deal with a conflict situation, do you say a prayer, incense the room, and pick up the phone? Request a face-to-face meeting in private? Ask a third party to mediate? However you deal with group or personal conflict in your so-called real life is key to knowing how to deal with it in your virtual life either as an individual or member of an online community.

Your church or mission-based organization has probably established norms for dealing with conflict in small groups (e.g., ministries, committees, councils, vestries). Use these to manage online conflict. Insight emerging from prayerful discernment should also help you decide when and how to intervene. Clarifying everything in written guidelines will make it easier to implement practical options that include:

> *Comment moderation:* Comments are how you stimulate conversation and build community on blogs. They're also where conflict and other bad behavior emerge. To mitigate that, posting a reminder for readers about maintaining civility, stating clearly which comments will be deleted, may help. Establishing comment moderation with registration required and/or a CAPTCHA code will filter out spambots. Decisions about commenting on, rejecting, or deleting comments should be made when creating a policy (see Appendix B: Yes, You Need a Social Media Policy).

> *Blocking:* All social media platforms include a mechanism for blocking people or organizations engaging in inappropriate behavior online. How swiftly you use this online deadly force will depend on whether the person is a "troll." This term is commonly used for anyone whose contributions to online conversations are always negative, combative, and inflammatory.

> *Back channel:* All social media platforms provide ways to connect privately, away from the public stream. In some instances, like on Twitter, you can only go through the

back channel to someone already following you or your organization. Don't forget email, texting, or phone as back channel means for reaching out.

No one should be surprised when conflict emerges within faith-based, God-loving, Christ-centered groups. It doesn't really matter if people come together because of shared beliefs, values, and goals; they'll end up in a scuffle about something. Corinthians come to my mind; how about yours?

On social media, as in daily life offline, we choose the lens that informs our vision. When it comes to social media, I suggest choosing to look through the lens of ministry and then answering Jesus' invitation to love one another.[37] Viewing social media as a tool for digital ministry means using it to minister and, more often than not, this includes reaching out really and virtually to those whose hurt and fear manifest as divisiveness.

THOUGHT BYTES

Prepare for managing inevitable, predictable online conflict by asking:

- How do we normally deal with conflict when it emerges in our community and ministries? Does this change if the person is relatively high profile?
- Does our social media policy provide guidelines for dealing with negative, disruptive, divisive, or downright nasty comments posted to our blogs and Facebook accounts?
- What sort of guidance about conflict management and resolution should we provide for whoever manages our social media accounts?

Chapter 26 Social Media Burnout

Social media will not work effectively if those using it for church communication are tired, frustrated, cranky, or apathetic because of it. These are signs of burnout, something long identified as an occupational hazard for ministers. Given the time, focus, and energy required for social media success, even experienced church communicators are susceptible.

I self-diagnosed my very own case of burnout the morning I burst into tears of relief rather than sobs of dismay at the sudden lack of internet connectivity. I was ready to reboot within hours but the experience forced me to look at what I was—or wasn't—doing to take care of myself. I wasn't taking care of myself, a long-standing pattern of behavior offline as well. No news there, alas.

While social media burnout is predictable, it need not be inevitable. In fact, social media might not be the problem. Since online behavior mirrors offline behavior, pay close attention to how you and your social media team—should you be blessed with a social media team—generally deal with intense highly focused, action-oriented activity.

The problem could be persistent patterns of behavior that include, but are not limited to, taking on more than can be accomplished reasonably well by a mere human being, diving into church activities without thinking through the time commitment, having difficulty delegating, or a not-so-latent desire for martyrdom.

If social media is, in fact, the problem, you can avert your untimely demise on it and sustain your church community's credible presence by:

- learning about and paying attention to symptoms of social media burnout (see box: Symptoms of Social Media Burnout, p. 108);
- clearly defining how much time you truly need to spend on your church's social media platforms;
- establishing systems to monitor the amount of time you spend on social media beyond what you've defined as ministry;
- using applications designed to make social media life easier and more manageable (see Chapter 21: Managing Social Media on Multiple Platforms);
- building social media Sabbaths and sabbaticals into your use, but don't disappear—let people know when you're taking a break; and
- developing a team to create and curate content, monitor and respond to content, and tweak accounts when functionality changes.

Although common wisdom dictates that we shouldn't go to the problem to solve the problem, social media actually does provide solutions to whatever problems it might generate.

Over the years, I've discovered that actively participating in or simply observing the antics of one online community can offset the fatigue of managing another. I've also been brought back from the brink of burnout by:

- chatting with church leaders who openly share frustrations, are mindful of their own risk for burnout, and who ask for as well as provide prayer support;
- attending prayer on Twitter;
- restoring my soul by scrolling through Pinterest boards of sacred images;

- listening to playlists of hymns on YouTube;
- following Twitterati who make gentle and sometimes not-so-gentle fun of grim piety; and
- subscribing to bloggers who openly explore what it means to be a person of faith in this broken world and messy church.

Symptoms of Social Media Burnout

Using social media to build community requires lots of time on a computer or smartphone. This can be mentally tiring and, depending on screen size and keyboard, physically taxing.

You probably already know the sure signs of computer fatigue (e.g., blurred vision, dry eyes, headaches, pains or cramps in hands or arms, lower back discomfort, sciatica). You're also probably familiar with standard ways to alleviate these symptoms (e.g., correcting ergonomics, scheduling breaks).

What about social media burnout?

Here I think it's useful to distinguish between being tired "from" and being tired "of" social media, although both emerge from overuse. You're heading for burnout if you once loved using social media and now:

- dread following accounts for yourself or anyone else;
- have significantly slowed down or completely stopped re-sponding to requests for information;
- let your posts devolve into snarky comments or shameless self-promotion;
- tend to undermine rather than participate in online conver-sations;
- ignore changes in functionality and terms of use affecting your account; and
- avoid reviewing your accounts for design, content, style, tone, and anything else that keeps them vibrantly up-to-date.

Alas, these easily recognizable symptoms of social media burnout are easily ignored. Holy God, Holy Mighty, Holy Immortal God, have mercy on those who ignore these.

As with everything else having to do with church and faith, prayerful discernment is at the core of sorting times for embracing from times for refraining. Instead of unplugging from all social media, first try using it to reinforce your devotional practices and receive support from people of faith. Use it to be a blessing to others. If that doesn't help, then turn the social media ministry over to someone else for a season before doing too much damage to self and others.

THOUGHT BYTES

Before pulling the plug on social media for yourself or your ministry, ask:

- Is social media helping to enhance my relationship with God or is it distracting me from my relationship with God?
- Do social media platforms help me serve and support others?
- Have I done everything I can to prevent social media burnout?

Chapter 27 Best Practices for Digital Ministry

Not even a decade on the scene and modern social media is now at a point where best practices have evolved. Best practices? This is the commonly used term for methods or techniques with a proven track record of working better than other methods or techniques.

I believe it's safe to say that all of the basic social media platforms have gone through many iterations in functionality and we're up to our second, if not third, generation of social media users. While still viewed with skepticism by some individuals and more insular types of organizations, communication professionals in the private, public, and nonprofit sectors now routinely include social media in their strategic plans. We know that social media platforms are must-have tools rather than digital toys no matter how much fun they may be to use. They sure are fun to use.

Social media has been tried and tested enough, especially in sectors whose concerns are issues similar to those within the world of church and faith (e.g., education, healthcare). Social media might be new to you and your church, but you do not have to invent best practices for using it. Best practices will continue evolving, but for now you can make social media work by following these guidelines:

- Ensure that whoever is in charge of digital ministry has access to and is invited to participate in program planning and decision making.

- Fully integrate social media into all other church communication plans.
- Ensure that whoever is involved with digital ministry is computer literate, comfortable with rapidly changing technology, and willing to learn whatever new web-based skills emerge.
- Develop a social media use policy that everyone, staff and volunteers, knows about, understands, and commits to using.
- Create a style guide to ensure continuity of editorial content across platforms.
- Create a brand book to ensure continuity of design, color palette, and images/logos across platforms.
- Properly credit all images and third-party content.
- Choose an easy-to-recognize name for social media accounts that best represents you or your organization.
- Include social media buttons, branded with each platform's recognizable logo on all communication materials.
- Generate a standardized list of tags, keywords, hashtags that staff and volunteers know about, understand, and commit to using.
- Designate one primary administrator for each social media account.
- Authorize at least two additional people to administer social media accounts.
- Create an editorial calendar for blog posts.
- Generate a set of sample tweets and Facebook posts as a reference for length and style.
- Balance content with conversation.
- Grant blog writing privileges to many, but grant blog editing privileges to only one person.
- Subscribe to and use a link-shortening service to conserve space and generate analytics.
- Choose and use an online service to manage multiple social media platforms.

- Choose and use an online service to schedule and automatically post social media content.
- Make sure anyone writing web content is trained in online-readable writing.
- Establish a review-and-approval process for blog posts and web content.
- Respond to all comments posted to/about social media content in near-real time.
- Establish a schedule for reviewing, tidying up, reconfiguring functionality and privacy settings for all social media accounts.
- "Pray without ceasing, give thanks in all circumstances" (1 Thess 5:17-18).

Appendix A   Strategic Choices

At first I was going to call this a list of "strategic decisions" but then remembered that thanks to the "cide" part, the word "decide" means to "kill off other options." Social media platforms offer so many options that I think it's more accurate to explore strategic *choices*. Note: I'm assuming you've *decided* to use social media and have killed off the option of ignoring it.

Tactical Issues

☐ How many social media networking sites can we comfortably and competently maintain?

☐ How many accounts within each platform can we comfortably and competently maintain?

☐ In whose name will accounts be opened and set up?

☐ Who will monitor our social media accounts? Should this be one person or a team? If it's a team, will we use initials to identify who is posting?

☐ Will we have group/institutional or individual
    ☐ blogs?
    ☐ Facebook pages?
    ☐ Twitter accounts?
    ☐ Pinterest boards?
    ☐ YouTube channels?

☐ Who will collect and safeguard all log-in information?

☐ How many people should have access to our social media accounts?

☐ How much authority to post content will be allowed to those with access to accounts?

☐ How frequently will we post content to each account?

☐ What percentage of original vs. curated content can or should we post?

☐ How many people and who will curate and create content?

☐ Who will create an editorial calendar for blog content?

☐ Who will review and copyedit blog content before it's posted?

☐ Do we want to schedule posts? If so, which service(s) will we use and who will monitor this?

☐ Who will ensure that images and messages, both in terms of design and content, are consistent across all platforms as well as our website?

☐ How will we monitor public conversations on social media relevant to our work as church?

Use Issues

What are our guidelines for:

☐ determining which type of content posts to each social media platform?

☐ deciding if and when to post the same content across platforms?

☐ participating in Twitter-based hashtag chats?

☐ interacting within our own denomination and reaching out to others?

☐ ensuring that content we create and curate reveals what it means to be Christ-centered and anchored in the Gospel?

Appendix B Yes, You Need a Social Media Policy

Not a month goes by in the world of church social media without someone tweeting a plea for examples of social media policies. A collective shudder ripples through the Twitterverse for two major reasons.

First, creating something useful and durable seems impossible because new platforms always emerge and existing ones change frequently.

Second, many question the need for such things. Shouldn't people of faith be trusted to use good judgment and act in alignment with professed faith? Do we need yet more institutionalized church bureaucracy? They chafe at the word policy, preferring that whatever gets created be called guidelines to deemphasize restricting and policing.[38] Here, to make everyone happy (as if that's ever possible) I'll use the words guidelines and policy interchangeably.

Onward.

Yes, you need social media guidelines, especially to manage multiple voices on multiple platforms. But be not afraid, the Lord and all those who have already created such policies are with you. The former is accessible by prayer, the latter via the internet. Ask via social media and you shall receive links to existing policies. With Google, most things are possible!

You'll have no problem finding existing guidelines you can adapt for your not-that-unique use. Really and truly, your organization is not unique. Read enough policies and you'll notice they're remarkably similar. Social media has been around long enough for standards to emerge.

Lucky for us who are keen on digital ministry, the challenge of defining and ensuring the appropriate use of social media has already been conquered by secular organizations facing similar safe-use issues. Don't limit your Google search to "church social media policies." Look at what schools, universities, hospital systems, and mission-based nonprofit organizations have put together, and then adapt those policies for church use.

Who should create these guidelines? This is one of the rare times I recommend putting together a team. It should include people who are active on social media and knowledgeable about how it works.

Because there's no need to reinvent anything, this process shouldn't take more than a month—okay, maybe two—if everyone stays focused. No one should be herded into a conference room to accomplish this task, certainly not one without snacks. Use Dropbox or Google Docs to circulate and revise drafts. No team? Consider engaging a consultant . . . who won't overcharge you.

The process is complete when the policy is finalized by whomever has that authority and everyone covered by the guidelines receives a copy and an orientation. You'll need snacks for that too.

If you want to start from semi-scratch, here's one way to organize the content of your social media policy:

Introduction

Sure, it's nice to have an overview about how social media has transformed the way we come together as a community of believers, but keep this section short. I've read some church social media policies where the preamble was theological rambling longer than the actual policy. Social media is brief and to the point; aim for that in this opening section.

Definitions

Set forth common terms as commonly used. If your policy covers other digital communications (e.g., e-newsletters, texting, email, mobile, wikis, chat rooms), then identify and define those as well.

Objectives

☐ Why are you establishing these policies?

☐ How will these policies benefit/protect employees, volunteers, and visitors to your social media sites?

Guiding Principles

☐ What values, beliefs, and ethics are at the foundation of your social media policy?

☐ Who has authority to speak for the organization?

Caution: Terms like "transparency" and "accountability" have now achieved the status of jargon, so if you use them you'll need to clarify what they mean.

Personal Privacy

☐ How are personal privacy rights defined?

☐ How will they be protected?

☐ How might social media infringe on those individual rights?

Confidentiality and Security

☐ How is confidentiality defined and how will it be ensured?

☐ What information is proprietary?

☐ What determines whether an account will be password protected?

☐ How often will passwords be changed?

☐ What are consequences of failing to manage and protect confidential information?

Note: Here's where you mention how anything published online is available to the public.

Practical Use and Scope

☐ Will the guidelines apply only to accounts set up by and for the organization?

☐ May employees and volunteers set up personal websites and social media accounts to support their ministries? If so, are those covered under the general policy?

☐ What needs to be included in user profiles?

☐ What constitutes inappropriate language and images?

☐ Under what conditions may adults interact with children/youth via social media?

☐ Under what conditions may vowed and/or ordained individuals interact with laity via social media?

☐ Will we have separate policies for each social media platform?

☐ When do employees and volunteers receive a copy of and orientation to the social media policy?

☐ Will we require employees and volunteers to sign a Verification Statement?

Note: You cannot control the internet.

Disclaimers

☐ Who is authorized to use social media accounts in an official capacity without including a disclaimer?

☐ What sorts of disclaimers need to be included on the bios/profiles/about field of personal social media accounts?

Legal Matters

☐ How will copyright, fair use, and IRS financial disclosure laws be honored?

☐ How will your organization honor secular reporting requirements for reporting of suspected abuse/neglect/exploitation of children, youth, elders, and vulnerable adults?

Emergency Use

☐ Which, if any, social media use guidelines are suspended in the event of a crisis, disaster, or emergency?

☐ What special guidelines go immediately into effect during a crisis, disaster, or emergency?

☐ What is your organization's definition of a crisis, disaster, or emergency?

Monitoring and Enforcement

☐ What is the process by which content is reviewed and approved?

☐ Should comment moderation be enabled on blogs?

☐ Under what circumstances should content—comments and postings—be removed by the account administrator(s)?

☐ How, how often, and for how long should records on social media accounts be kept?

☐ How will these guidelines be enforced?

☐ What are the consequences of noncompliance?

☐ Have we clarified civil or criminal penalties as provided by law?

☐ Have we clarified penalties as provided by church canon law/ norms/rubrics?

Provide Samples of:

☐ Disclaimer for Personal Social Media Sites (boilerplate)

☐ Disclaimer for Institutional Social Media Sites (boilerplate)

☐ Media Release Form

☐ Verification Statement for Employees/Volunteers to sign

For Examples, See:

Evangelical Lutheran Church in America, *Social Media and Congregations*, http://bit.ly/JrL47X

United Methodist Communications, *Social Media for Churches*, http://bit.ly/11Z1WJh

United States Conference of Catholic Bishops, *Social Media Guidelines*, http://bit.ly/TEbN1t

Appendix C The Communications Audit

"So where do we start?"

I'm most frequently asked this question in emails, on the phone, and during social media workshops. Everyone seems shocked when I vehemently suggest starting with a communications audit before doing anything else different or new.

In reality, I already know they'll probably need to redo their website and set up social media accounts but in my never-ending quest to work within best practices, I always recommend an audit to assess whether existing materials are consistent, coherent, and on target. Generally they are not. Plus, should a strategic plan for communications exist, an audit will reveal whether goals are being met. In the absence of an existing plan, an audit will identify gaps and clarify needs so an actionable plan can be created.

Optimally, a communications audit should be done by someone qualified to review and analyze everything created and used by a church/organization to communicate with all audiences.

Everything = print, digital, broadcast.

All audiences = internal as well as external.

Your auditor must be able to interview everyone involved with creating and using materials to tease out information about what works, what doesn't, and what could work better. Your auditor must be able to keep an eye on the prize (i.e., big picture) and love working with details because a comprehensive audit involves:

- assessing consistency and continuity of message, content, and design within and among materials;
- identifying inconsistencies and redundancies within and among materials;
- recommending ways to consolidate and/or eliminate materials to reduce costs; and
- proposing next steps for taking action and a timetable for their completion.

None of this can happen without full cooperation up and down the church management food chain because if you agree to an audit, you'll have to provide copies of all:

☐ printed materials including but not limited to publications, collateral materials (e.g., flyers, posters, mailings, brochures);

☐ printed materials used to identify your church/organization (e.g., stationery, business cards, name tags, decals, banners);

☐ images and logos;

☐ broadcast media (e.g., radio and television announcements);

☐ written plans or memoranda outlining plans or requests for communications relative to mission, vision, identity, special projects, and any other initiatives;

☐ budgets created for general and department-specific communication efforts;

☐ existing policies relative to communication; and

☐ current style guides and brand books.

You'll also need to provide:

☐ URLs for online materials created and used by everyone in the church/organization including but not limited to the website and social media (e.g., blogs, Facebook pages, Twitter, YouTube, LinkedIn); and

☐ samples of e-newsletters and email blasts.

When I perform an audit, I ask the chief communications person (or beleaguered soul stuck with picking up communication slack) to prepare a brief memo outlining the top three goals, priorities, and needs.

I also request that all crooked paths be made straight so I may and can have confidential conversations with everyone on staff, including those in charge of finances. Frankly, I love talking with finance people for two major reasons: (1) they're grateful to be included for a change; and (2) I *always* find out where costs can be cut and money can be saved. And because it took me a while to realize this could not be assumed, I insist that the most senior person (i.e., pastor, bishop) be involved with the interview process and receive a copy of the final report.

Sound like a lot of work? It is!

Still, a full audit can be completed relatively quickly if and when you provide unimpeded access to materials, staff, and, in some instances, outside vendors. Again, completing a communications audit is an essential first step, especially if the final report is used as a checklist of things to get done and if there's a genuine commitment to move forward. Alas, sometimes there isn't, but that sorry truth will also come out during an audit.

Notes

Note: Bit.ly is a URL shortening service that eliminates the need to write out über-long URLs. These codes are case sensitive, which means they need to by typed in exactly. If you get an error code, it's probably because you've typed a numeral one (1) instead of a lower letter el (l) or a zero (0) instead of a capital (O) or a lower case letter el (l) instead of a capital I (I). It's really not this complicated but sometimes the style of printed fonts can cause confusion. If you're reading this on an e-reader, you just click on the hot link.

1. "Early adopters" is the term used to describe crazies who jump in and try new technologies, usually in beta (i.e., first iteration before it goes public). I will not reveal which social media platforms I've explored in beta on the grounds that I can't remember all of them. I will admit that despite my adoration of Twitter, I'm only a quasi-early adopter. It was publicly introduced July 15, 2006. I joined on October 14, 2008. Observers tend to agree that Twitter became noticeably popular among techies during the 2007 South by Southwest Interactive (SXSWi) conference.

2. Thanks to the way social media has messed with *chronos*, I think having a five-year plan for communication makes no sense. Everything you'd accomplish in five years with traditional media tools will take only one to three years with social media and other digital tools.

3. I include myself among those who use this verse from the Gospel of John. It's irresistible and unavoidable. I used it to open a chapter in *The Word Made Fresh: Communicating Church and Faith Today*, vowed I wouldn't do so again and, well, here I am, citing it.

4. For examples of the more advanced theological discussions about social media, digital ministry, and "digital ecclesiology" that are currently emerging, visit and explore the New Media Project website http://

www.cpx.edu/10pocNX and search online for work by Elizabeth Dre-
scher, PhD, who teaches, speaks, and publishes extensively on this
topic. On the #chsocm blog, you'll find a post by the Rev. David L.
Hansen titled "Virtual Faith, Incarnational Community," http://www.cpx
.edu/NKR2Ef, that framed this conversation for the September 4, 2012
tweetchat he moderated (http://www.cpx.edu/10pqzQT).

5. "Prayer for Technology: Christ Has No Online Presence . . ."
posted to YouTube on October 28, 2012, by Cheryl Smith: http://bit
.ly/10puMUT.

6. Second Life is a 3D virtual world launched in June 2003. Users
create and then interact through avatars. The avatars may or may not
reflect who or what users are in their "first" life. By 2008, nearly 100
churches were set up on Second Life. For a list of churches on Second
Life as of February 2010, see "Anglican and Other Churches in Second
Life" posted to CDBurt (C. David Burt's Website): http://bit.ly/W7yLyk.
For a discussion of churches in virtual worlds, see Stefan Gelfgren,
"Virtual Churches, Participatory Culture, and Secularization," *Journal
of Technology, Theology, & Religion* 2, no. 1 (January 2011): http://bit
.ly/W7ymMu.

7. The Rev. Ed Kay in email correspondence with author on December 23, 2012: "My test for thinking about/using things theologically is
look at 'X' through a God-lens." We started the conversation on Twitter
and moved it to email because that's how #chsocm chat folks roll!

8. For a more detailed explanation of how this list of demographic
variables has remained stable even though terms and their meanings
have shifted, please read pages 32 through 41 in my earlier book about
church communication: *The Word Made Fresh: Communicating Church
and Faith Today* (Harrisburg, PA: Morehouse, 2008).

9. William Strauss and Neil Howe are the theorists most frequently
cited for their work about generations, starting with *Generations: The
History of America's Future, 1584 to 2069* (New York: William Morrow,
1991). Douglas Coupland is credited for naming Generation X in his
novel *Generation X: Tales for an Accelerated Culture* (New York: St.
Martin's Press, 1991). I'm a big fan of Gail Sheehy's work in *Passages:
Predictable Crises of Adult Life* (New York: E. P. Dutton, 1976) and *New
Passages: Mapping Your Life Across Time* (New York: Ballantine, 1995).

10. There's lots of publicly available data about how social media
use is distributed across generations, some of the most credible being
from the Pew Internet Project and the major marketing research firms.

If you want to study this in more detail, a Google search for "how different generations use social media" will help you find what's out there.

11. Jakob Nielsen, "Participation Inequality: Encouraging More Users to Contribute," Alertbox, October 9, 2006, http://bit.ly/10pa3Ay.

12. Adapted from #chsocm tweetchat transcript, August 28, 2012, http://bit.ly/10p6hqJ.

13. Your integration into community shifts into high gear the moment anyone in church leadership discovers your sought-after skill set. Changed in a moment, in the twinkling of an eye before the last trumpet you will be put in charge of something and everyone shall know and call you by name.

14. "'Nones' on the Rise: One-in-Five Adults Have No Religious Affiliation," The Pew Forum on Religion & Public Life, October 9, 2012, http://bit.ly/U3tMkC.

15. No need to reinvent any wheels. Studying how the healthcare industry, education sector, and nonprofit organizations have used social media will provide insights about strategy and practical application. Freely copping to shameless self-promotion, I recommend reading this book about healthcare social media that I contributed to and edited: Mayo Clinic Center for Social Media, *Bringing the Social Media #Revolution to Health Care* (Rochester, MN: Mayo Foundation for Medical Education and Research, 2012).

16. Charlene Li, "Forrester's new Social Technographics report," *Empowered*, April 23, 2007, http://bit.ly/RQA7Pk.

17. Josh Bernoff, "Social Technographics: Conversationalists get onto the ladder," *Empowered*, January 19, 2010, http://bit.ly/RaYGUl.

18. See #chsocm tweetchat transcript for September 6, 2011: http://bit.ly/10pNuvp.

19. Impossible to find on the Microsoft site, the article by Bill Gates titled "Content is King" has been reproduced by blogger Craig Bailey at http://bit.ly/W9OHQB (May 31, 2010).

20. Current data from Pew indicates that content creation and curation seem to be almost evenly distributed among adults online who use social media platforms. Joanna Brenner, "Pew Internet: Social Networking," Pew Internet & American Life Project, February 14, 2013, http://bit.ly/10pPTpV.

21. Kathryn Zickuhr and Aaron Smith, "Digital Differences," Pew Internet & American Life Project, April 13, 2012, http://bit.ly/VyYJv3.

22. Matthew 11:21.

23. For comprehensive, well-documented history of blogs and blogging, see this Wikipedia entry: http://en.wikipedia.org/wiki/Blog. Yes, it's possible to find accurate, rigorous information on Wikipedia. Don't judge me.

24. Deacon Jim Knipper, *Teach What You Believe: Musings, Commentary, and Other Thought Fodder from a Roman Catholic Deacon* (blog), http://bit.ly/wVpl0y.

25. Isaiah 55:11.

26. See Penny Nash, "Facebook Basics: It's All About the News Feed," August 11, 2011, http://bit.ly/qN58IZ.

27. Inside Facebook, http://bit.ly/12YBpgo.

28. Facebook changes so frequently that I could not resist using this title for a post about it on the church social media (#chsocm) blog: "Another Week, Another Facebook Tweak," September 26, 2011, http://bit.ly/n586A6.

29. Lauren Dugan, "Facebook, Twitter, Google+, Pinterest: The Users of Social Media," All Twitter (Media Bistro), May 15, 2012, http://bit.ly/W9Os8i.

30. Meredith Gould, writer, editor, and producer, "Social Media: Don't Be That Church," posted to YouTube on July 17, 2011, http://bit.ly/TPVRIx.

31. Meredith Gould, writer, editor, and producer, "Don't Be That Church II: We Need a New Website," posted to YouTube on October 7, 2012, http://bit.ly/TPWzFy.

32. #chsocm chat, September 18, 2012, http://bit.ly/VHv8OL.

33. For an articulate discussion of arguments against making evangelism another form of marketing, see Tyler Wigg-Stevenson, "Jesus Is Not a Brand," *Christianity Today*, January 2, 2009, http://bit.ly/12jytd4.

34. If you don't know how to do this, search Google to find directions. Don't bother searching Google to find directions for using breviary ribbons. I already did, there aren't any.

35. Most chats begin with five to ten minutes of self-introductions, followed by forty minutes of moderated chatting about two to four topics. The weekly #chsocm chat always opens with prayer and ends with an antiphon from Compline, which I believe has helped establish the friendly, generous tone of the chat.

36. Terms for structure require translation when working ecumenically. What Roman Catholics and Episcopalians/Anglicans call a "diocese" is termed a "synod" among Lutherans. For more translations, see

Meredith Gould, "Church Structure Found in Translation," in *The Word Made Fresh: Communicating Church and Faith Today* (Harrisburg, PA: Morehouse, 2008), 52.

37. John 15:9-17.

38. Word to the wise: do not waste precious energy trying to guess who (e.g., clergy, lay leadership, church administrators, church communication pros) ends up on which side of this debate.

Subject Index

Scripture Index